COPYRIGHT

© Copyright 2024 My Wedding Songs

Published in the United States by WeddingMuseum LLC dba My Wedding Songs

All Rights Reserved. No part of this publication may be reproduced, distributed, or transmitted in any form or by any means, including, but not limited to, photocopying, recording, or other electronic or mechanical methods, without the prior written permission of the publisher, except for the use of brief quotations in a book review. If you would like permission, please contact the publisher at hello@myweddingsongs.com.

ISBN: 9798340755292

Second Edition.

To start planning your wedding music online, visit MyWeddingSongs.com.

Join the Wedding MusicLetter for the latest and trending wedding songs - every Wednesday.

TABLE OF CONTENTS

Copyright - 1
Table of Contents - 2
How To Plan Your Wedding Songs - 3

Greatest Wedding Songs All Time - 4
Trending Songs - 5
Modern Love Songs - 6

Wedding Ceremony

Prelude Songs - 7-8
Groom Processional Songs - 9
Wedding Party Processional Songs - 10
Bride Processional Songs - 11
Unity Ceremony Songs - 12
Memorial Songs - 13
Recessional Songs - 14

Wedding Reception

Cocktail Hour Songs - 15
Entrance & Intro Songs - 16
First Dance Songs - 17
Dinner Music - 18
Cake Cutting Songs - 19
Father-Figure Dance - 20
Mother-Figure Dance - 21
Mother-Daughter Songs - 22
Father-Son Songs - 23
Combined Parent Dance - 24
Step-Parents Songs - 25
In-Law Dance Songs - 26
Bridesmaids Songs - 27
Groomsmen Songs - 28
Sister Songs - 29
Sister Brother Songs - 30
Brother Songs - 31
Wedding Party Dance Songs - 32
Anniversary Dance Songs - 33
Bouquet Toss Songs - 34
Garter Removal Songs - 35
Garter Toss Songs - 36
Garter Placement Songs - 37
Party Songs - 38
Slow Songs - 39
Money Dance Songs - 40
Line Dance Songs - 41
Last Dance Songs - 42
Private Last Dance Songs - 43

Eras

1950s Wedding Songs - 44
1960s Wedding Songs - 45
1970s Wedding Songs - 46
1980s Wedding Songs - 47
1990s Wedding Songs - 48
2000s Wedding Songs - 49
2010s Wedding Songs - 50

Genres & Misc

Afrobeats Wedding Songs - 51
Christian Wedding Songs - 52
Classic Rock Love Songs - 53
Country Wedding Songs - 54
Disco Wedding Songs - 55
EDM/Dance Wedding Songs - 56-57
Folk Wedding Songs - 58
Hip Hop Wedding Songs - 59
Indie Wedding Songs - 60
Instrumental Wedding Songs - 61
Jazz Wedding Songs - 62
Latin Wedding Songs - 63
LGBTQ+ Wedding Songs - 64
Motown Wedding Songs - 65
Pop Wedding Songs - 66
Pop-Punk Wedding Songs - 67
R&B Wedding Songs - 68
Reggae Wedding Songs - 69
Rock Wedding Songs - 70
Sing-along Songs - 71
Texas Country & Red Dirt Songs - 72

Wedding Music Details - 73
Wedding Details - 74
Wedding Planning Notes - 75

About the Author - 76

Note: Each playlist has a QR Code to listen on Spotify.

Join the Wedding MusicLetter for the latest and trending wedding songs - every Wednesday.

HOW TO PLAN YOUR WEDDING SONGS

How do I pick songs for my wedding day?
First and foremost, select songs that mean something to you. If you are a big *Star Wars* fan, then play "The Imperial March" as you walk down the aisle. If there was a song playing during your first date that has a special meaning, play it as your first dance.

What is the order of events during a wedding day?
The order of song lists in this planner for the wedding ceremony and reception are in the common order of events. However, you can choose to change the order. For example, if you do not want to have your first dance immediately following your grand entrance, you can choose to have it after the meal.

Should you incorporate traditional wedding songs, modern songs, or personal favorites?
The music selected may be limited to the location of the event. Some locations, such as churches, may have strict guidelines as to what can be played. You can incorporate your music tastes into a ceremony through instrumental cover songs and acoustic covers. As for the reception, have a themed cocktail hour and dinner music such as a tropical house playlist, bossa nova playlist, or yacht rock playlist. As a baseline, don't bore guests which results in them leaving early.

Should you have a mix of slow and fast songs for the reception?
Yes. Select a few slow songs too so that you offer the opportunity for cherished moments at your reception. Give an Aunt, Uncle, or Grandparent (any relative or friend) a chance to dance with someone they are close to or don't get to see often.

What type of music should I pick for my reception?
Start with music you like but also with your fiance, family, and friends. When the reception doors open is the time to play a wide range of eras and genres. The music should start with your suggestions but also experiment with known crowd pleasers. The music entertainment can get a feel for what guests are grooving to, singing along to, and tapping their toes to. Typically a reception will start with older hits and move to more modern hits as the event progresses.

How do I use this guide?
This guide is meant to help lead the way to select music for your wedding day. You will find popular selections, hidden gems, and unique tracks. Circle the songs you want to be played and cross off the "do not play". Then, create your playlist on Spotify or give it to your DJ or band so that they know what songs you want. But, give it to them 3-4 weeks before your wedding so that they can prepare an optimal mixable setlist.

Join the Wedding MusicLetter for the latest and trending wedding songs - every Wednesday.

THE GREATEST

Ceremony
A Thousand Years – Christina Perri
At Last – Etta James
Can't Help Falling In Love – Elvis Presley
From The Ground Up – Dan + Shay
From This Moment On – Shania Twain
Here Comes The Sun - Beatles
I Get To Love You – Ruelle
Marry Me – Train
Signed, Sealed, Delivered I'm Yours – Stevie Wonder
This Will Be (An Everlasting Love) – Natalie Cole
You Make My Dreams – Daryl Hall & John Oates

Entrance & Introductions
I Gotta Feeling – Black Eyed Peas
Let's Get Married – Jagged Edge

Cocktail Hour & Dinner
Be My Baby – The Ronettes
Can We Talk – Tevin Campbell
Dancing in the Moonlight – King Harvest
Fast Car – Luke Combs
How Sweet It Is (To Be Loved By You) – Taylor or Gaye
Lovely Day – Bill Withers
What's Up? – 4 Non Blondes
You Are The Best Thing – Ray Lamontagne

First Dance
All Of Me – John Legend
Beyond – Leon Bridges
I Don't Want To Miss A Thing – Aerosmith
I Will Always Love You – Whitney Houston
Lover – Taylor Swift
Perfect – Ed Sheeran
Thank God – Kane Brown & Katelyn Brown

Parents Dances
I Hope You Dance – Lee Ann Womack
Isn't She Lovely – Stevie Wonder
My Girl – The Temptations
My Wish – Rascal Flatts
Over The Rainbow – Israel Kamakawiwo'ole
What A Wonderful World – Louis Armstrong

Bouquet Toss
Single Ladies (Put A Ring On It) – Beyonce

Dancing
A Bar Song (Tipsy) – Shaboozey
Ain't No Mountain High Enough – Gaye, Terrell
Boogie Shoes – KC and the Sunshine Band
Brown Eyed Girl – Van Morrison
Can't Get Enough – Tamia
Can't Hold Us – Macklemore & Ryan Lewis
Can't Stop The Feeling! – Justin Timberlake
Candy - Cameo
Celebration – Kool & The Gang
Cha Cha Slide – Mr C
Cupid Shuffle – Cupid
Dancing Queen – ABBA
Danza Kuduro – Don Omar feat. Lucenzo
DJ Got Us Fallin' In Love – Usher
Everybody (Backstreet's Back) – Backstreet Boys
Fireball – Pitbull feat. John Ryan
Friends In Low Places – Garth Brooks
Good Feeling – Flo Rida
Hey Ya! – Outkast
Hips Don't Lie – Shakira feat. Wyclef Jean
I Had Some Help – Post Malone feat. Morgan Wallen
I Wanna Dance With Somebody – Whitney Houston
I'm Good (Blue) – David Guetta & Bebe Rexha
In Da Club – 50 Cent
Jerusalema – Master KG feat. Nomcebo Zikode
Jump Around – House Of Pain
Let's Get Loud – Jennifer Lopez
Let's Stay Together – Al Green
Lil Boo Thang – Paul Russell
Livin' On A Prayer – Bon Jovi
Low – Flo Rida feat. T-Pain
Man! I Feel Like A Woman! – Shania Twain
Mr. Brightside – The Killers
No Hands – Waka Flocka Flame
Party In The U.S.A. – Miley Cyrus
Pepas – Farruko
Play That Funky Music – Wild Cherry
September – Earth, Wind & Fire
Seven Nation Army – The White Stripes
Shake It Off (Taylor's Version) – Taylor Swift
Shivers – Ed Sheeran
Shout – The Isley Brothers/Otis Day
Shut Up And Dance – Walk The Moon
Stand By Me – Ben E. King
Sweet Caroline – Neil Diamond
Tennessee Whiskey – Chris Stapleton
The Middle – Jimmy Eat World
This Is How We Do It – Montell Jordan
TiK ToK – Kesha
Timber – Pitbull feat. Kesha
Time of Our Lives – Pitbull & Ne-Yo
Titanium – David Guetta feat. Sia
Turn Down for What – DJ Snake, Lil Jon
Until I Found You – Stephen Sanchez
Unwritten – Natasha Bedingfield
Uptown Funk – Mark Ronson, Bruno Mars
Wagon Wheel – Darius Rucker/Old Crow Medicine Show
Wake Me Up – Avicii
Wannabe – Spice Girls
We Are Family – Sister Sledge
We Found Love – Rihanna, Calvin Harris
Wobble – V.I.C.
Yeah! – Usher, Ludacris, Lil' Jon

Last Dance
Don't Stop Believin' – Journey
Take Me Home, Country Roads – John Denver

Join the Wedding MusicLetter for the latest and trending wedding songs - every Wednesday.

TRENDING SONGS

Trending Backtracks
Always Be My Baby – Mariah Carey
Breakin' Dishes – Rihanna
Call Me Maybe – Carly Rae Jepsen
Crazy – Gnarls Barkley
Die Young – Kesha
Dog Days Are Over – Florence + The Machine
Don't Give Up on Me – Andy Grammer
Electric Avenue – Eddy Grant
Fire Woman – The Cult
Good Feeling – Flo Rida
I Want It That Way – Backstreet Boys
Live Like You Were Dying – Tim McGraw
Out of My League – Fitz & The Tantrums
Rather Be – Clean Bandit feat. Jess Glynne
Rhythm Is A Dancer – Snap!
Since U Been Gone – Kelly Clarkson
Smooth – Santana, Rob Thomas
Titanium – David Guetta Feat. Sia
Toxic – Britney Spears
Unwritten – Natasha Bedingfield
Walking On A Dream – Empire Of The Sun
We Are Young – Fun. feat. Janelle Monáe
What Dreams Are Made Of – Hilary Duff
What's Up? – 4 Non Blondes
When Doves Cry – Prince
You Belong With Me (Taylor's Version) – Taylor Swift
You're The One That I Want – J. Travolta, O. Newton-John

New Party & Dancing Songs
360 – Charli XCX
A Bar Song (Tipsy) – Shaboozey
Austin (Boots Stop Workin') – Dasha
Dance The Night – Dua Lipa
Hang Tight Honey – Lainey Wilson
HOT UPTOWN – Camila Cabello feat. Drake
Houdini – Eminem
I Don't Wanna Wait – David Guetta & OneRepublic
I Had Some Help – Post Malone feat. Morgan Wallen
I'm Good (Blue) – David Guetta, Bebe Rexha
Lil Boo Thang – Paul Russell
Lovin On Me – Jack Harlow
Miles On It – Marshmello & Kane Brown
Million Dollar Baby – Tommy Richman
My Oh My – Ava Max
Not Like Us – Kendrick Lamar
Omg – Candelita
Pour Me A Drink – Post Malone feat. Blake Shelton
Shake Dat Ass (Twerk Song) – BossMan Dlow
Shivers – Ed Sheeran
Si Antes Te Hubiera Conocido – KAROL G
Sunshine (My Girl) – Wuki
TEXAS HOLD 'EM – Beyoncé
Whatever – Kygo & Ava Max
Where The Party At – Lacee

New Mid-Tempo Songs
After Hours – Kehlani
Beautiful Things – Benson Boone
BIRDS OF A FEATHER – Billie Eilish
Carry You Home – Alex Warren
Espresso – Sabrina Carpenter
Fast Car – Luke Combs
Flowers – Miley Cyrus
Fortnight – Taylor Swift feat. Post Malone
GO HOME W U – Keith Urban & Lainey Wilson
GOOD DAY – Forrest Frank
HERicane – Lucky Daye
Houdini – Dua Lipa
II MOST WANTED – Beyoncé & Miley Cyrus
Last Night – Morgan Wallen
Lose Control – Teddy Swims
Lost In Space – Foster The People
Love Me JeJe – Tems
Music On The Radio – Empire Of The Sun
Paint The Town Red – Doja Cat
Please Please Please – Sabrina Carpenter
Riptide – TWOPILOTS
So In Love – Lalah Hathaway
Stargazing – Myles Smith
THESE ARE THE DAYS – Niko Moon
Til You Can't – Cody Johnson
Too Sweet – Hozier
Your Love Is All I Need – Vedo

Trending Slow Songs
All I Want Is You – The Decemberists
Beautiful Crazy – Luke Combs
Fade Into You – Mazzy Star
Fantasmas – Humbe
Good Riddance (Time of Your Life) – Green Day
I Choose You – Forest Blakk
In Your Love – Tyler Childers
Made For Me – Muni Long
Paradise – Justin Timberlake feat. *Nsync
Save Me – Jelly Roll with Lainey Wilson
The Scientist – Coldplay

New Ceremony Songs
A Whole New World – R. Gromes & Julian Riem
Always Remember Us This Way – Enrique Lázaro
Fall Into Me – Maneli Jamal
In Case You Didn't Know (Piano Version) – Brett Young
Kiss the Rain – HAUSER
Levels – Midnite String Quartet
Nothing Else Matters – HarpistKT
The Prayer (Piano Version) – Pardon my Piano
This Is What You Came For – Lars Florence
Wonderwall – Thousand Impressions

Join the Wedding MusicLetter for the latest and trending wedding songs - every Wednesday.

MODERN LOVE SONGS

10-90 – Muscadine Bloodline
24/7, 365 – Elijah Woods
4 Me – Don Toliver, Kali Uchis
A Love Like This – New Kids On The Block
A Night To Remember – beabadoobee, Laufey
Ain't Love Somethin' – Sam Booker
All I Want Is You – The Decemberists
All the Way – Shane Smith & the Saints
All the Ways – The Secret Sisters, Ray LaMontagne
As a matter of fact – Babyface
At Your Worst – Calum Scott
Baby Will You Love Me – MAJOR.
Be The One – Bree Runway & Khalid
Before I Met You – Dana Powell
Best Friend – Pacific Skyway
BIRDS OF A FEATHER – Billie Eilish
Breathe – Caleb and Kelsey
Can't Get Enough Of Your Love, Babe – Jason Morales
Choose You – Elmiene
Country Gold – Anne Wilson, Jordan Davis
Dance With You – Brett Young
Evergreen – Teddy Swims
Everything to Me – Ivan & Alyosha
First Dancin' – 2 Lane Summer
Forest Blakk – I Choose You (Wedding Version)
Forever – Ash B
Forever – Noah Kahan
Forever To Me – Cole Swindell
From The Jump (Duet Version) – Arthur, Clarkson
God Made You – 2 Lane Summer
Gonna Love You – Parmalee
Good Together – Lake Street Drive
Heaven – Cleo Sol
Highs & Lows – Chance Peña
Holding You – David McCredie
I'm Gonna Love You – Josh Tatofi
If You Were Mine – Miranda Lambert & Leon Bridges
In My Arms – Billy Raffoul
In Your Love – Tyler Childers
Landed – Ruelle, Aron Wright
Let's Fall In Love – Raheem DeVaughn
Life With You – Kelsey Hart
Lighthouse – Calum Scott
LOML – Shaé Universe
Lost in You (Remix) – Jade Novah & Kevin Ross
Love Can Be – Rebecca Rea
Love Is – Ingrid Michaelson & Jason Mraz
Love Me For The Both Of Us – CJ Fam
Love You Anyway – Devon Gilfillian
Loved By You – Simone Torres

Made (Wedding Version) – Spencer Crandall
Made For Me – Muni Long
Magical – Ed Sheeran
marry me – KANII
Morning Sun – Otis Kane
My Feet Don't Touch the Ground – Bonner Rhae
Never Change – BJ The Chicago Kid, Philip Bailey
Never Giving up on You – Frankie J
Nobody But You – JLake
Nobody Else – Dave Thomas Junior
NOTHING NEW (I DO) – Brandon Lake
Nothing's Gonna Change My Love For You – MTL, Drilon
Now I Do – Bailey Taylor
Oh My – Fireboy Dml
One of Mine – Drew Green
Pancakes & Butter – Jason Mraz
Paradise – Justin Timberlake feat. *NSYNC
Perfect For Me – Bradley Marshall
Perfect to Me – Josh Tatofi
perfectly imperfect – Yung Crusha & Beautiful Beats
Promise You That – Trevor Martin
Rest of Your Life – David J
Risk It All – Usher, H.E.R.
So Glad I Found You – Jalen Ngonda
Space In My Heart – Enrique Iglesias, Miranda Lambert
Spin You Around (1/24) – Morgan Wallen
Stupid In Love [Stripped Version] – MAX, HUH YUNJIN
superglue – joan
Sweet Talk – Iron & Wine
Take Forever (Hally's Song) – Cooper Alan
That Part – Lauren Spencer Smith
That's You – Lucky Daye
The Day That I Met You – Matilda Mann
The Mountain Song (First Dance Version) – Tophouse
Timber! – The National Parks
Time With You – Johnny and Heidi
Too Good to be True – Kacey Musgraves
Under That Veil – Christian Keyes
Waiting On You – Jon B, Tank
Waterfall (I Adore You) – Yebba
way after forever – Vaultboy
Whatcha Done Now – Leela James
When It Comes To You – Fridayy
When We First Met – Emmit Fenn
Who I Am With You – Tucker Beathard
You – Eric Roberson
You – Omar Cunningham
You Plus Me – Plain White T's
You're the One – Rhiannon Giddens
Your Hands – Mae Estes

PRELUDE SONGS I

Traditional Classical
A Rose Is Gently Blooming – Meral Guneyman
Air on G (Arr. for Violin and Acoustic Guitar by Arthur Campbell) – Anne Akiko Meyers, Jason Vieaux
Air on the G String – HAUSER
Arioso (Adagio in G) from Cantata BWV 156 (Arr. by Lloyd Webber) – J.S. Bach
Ave Maria, D.839 – Arr. Hazell – Sheku Kanneh-Mason
Bagatelle in A Minor, WoO 59, "Fur Elise" – Ludwig van Beethoven
Canon In D (Guitar) – The O'Neill Brothers Group
Canon In F – The O'Neill Brothers Group
Cello Suite No. 1 in G Major, BWV 1007: I. Prélude – João Kouyoumdjian
Cello Suite No. 1 in G Major, Prélude – Yo-Yo Ma
Clair de Lune, L. 32 – Martin Jones
Etude No. 2 – Philip Glass
Für Elise, WoO 59 – Nelly Kokinos
Holy, Holy, Holy, Lord God Almighty (Wedding Hymn) – Robbins Island Music Group
Pachelbel's Canon in D – Danny Wright
Prelude in C Major – Brian Bradley
Rockelbel's Canon (Pachelbel's Canon in D) – The Piano Guys
Romance for String Orchestra, Op. 11 – Academy of St Martin in the Fields
Romantic Pieces, Op. 75, B. 150 – 1. Allegro moderato – Akiko Suwanai
Salut d'Amour, Op. 12 – Yo-Yo Ma
Sarabande, BWV 1007 – Andrei Krylov & Lana Ross
Sheep May Safely Graze – Leon Fleisher
Sleepers Awake, Wachet Auf, Ruft Uns Die Stimme, BWV 140 – Andrei Krylov & Lana Ross
Suite bergamasque, L. 75 – III. Clair de lune – Lang Lang, Claude Debussy
The Four Seasons, Violin Concerto in E Major, Op. 8 No. 1, RV 269 "Spring": I. Allegro – Itzhak Perlman
The Occasional Oratorio, HWV62 – George Frideric Handel
Trumpet Tune in C Major, Z. 697 – The Prague Brass Soloists
Trumpet Voluntary in D Major "The Prince of Denmark's March" – The Clerkenwell Baroque String
Water Music Suite, HWV 348-350 – Hornpipe – Wolfgang Meyer, Berlin Philharmonic, Rafael Kubelik

Join the Wedding MusicLetter for the latest and trending wedding songs - every Wednesday.

PRELUDE SONGS II

Modern Covers
A Thousand Years – The Piano Guys
A Thousand Years – VioDance
Back At One (Instrumental Cover) - Johan Sander
Bittersweet Symphony – Vitamin String Quartet
Can't Help Falling In Love – Amber Leigh Irish
Enchanted - Midnite String Quartet
Enchanted (The Wedding Violin Version) - Ana Done
Faithfully - Laura Sullivan
First Day of My Life – Brooklyn Duo
God Bless the Broken Road – O'Neill Brothers Group
golden hour - Brooklyn Duo
Here Comes the Sun – Benny Martin
I Get To Love You - Brooklyn Duo
I'm Yours (Guitar Version) - Mount Hayes
In My Life – Kevin Kern
Kiss From A Rose – Vitamin String Quartet
Kiss the Rain - HAUSER
Latch – Simply Three
Love Me Like You Do – Brooklyn Duo
Love Story Instrumental Piano - Roman Tee
Lover – Paul Hankinson Covers
Marry You – The O'Neill Brothers Group
My Boo (Acoustic) – Will Gittens, Rahky
Pachelbel Meets U2 – Jon Schmidt
Perfect – Paul Hankinson Covers
Say You Won't Let Go – Daniel Jang
Shape Of My Heart - The Piano Guys
Somewhere Only We Know – Simply Three
Stand By Me – Fred Turnquist
Sunflower – Vitamin String Quartet ft. ThatViolaKid
This Is What You Came For - Lars Florence
This Will Be (An Everlasting Love) – Dr. Cover Band
Truly Madly Deeply - Sidney
Turning Page (Instrumental) – Sleeping At Last
Wildest Dreams – Dallas String Quartet
Yellow (Piano Version) – Henry Smith

Video Games, Plays, TV & Film
A Million Dreams (Piano Version) – Emilie's Piano
A Whole New World – Disney Ukulele & Disney
All I Ask Of You - Andrew Lloyd Webber
Ashitaka and San (Princess Mononoke) – CelloKat
Beauty and the Beast – Disney Ukulele & Disney
Concerning Hobbits – Howard Shore
Fairy Tail Theme – Taylor Davis, Lara De Wit
Game of Thrones (Main Theme) – Vitamin String Quartet
Hold My Hand – Alexandre Pachabezian
If I Ain't Got You (Orchestral) - Alicia Keys
Married Life from Up (Violin & Piano) – Paul Hankinson
Reveries – Ramin Djawadi
Rewrite The Stars (Piano Version) – Emilie's Piano
Seasons Of Love (RENT) – Stan Whitmire
The Princess Bride – Storybook Love – VSQ

Modern Romance
Ain't Love Somethin - Sam Brooker
At Your Worst (Acoustic) - Calum Scott
Best Part – H.E.R., Daniel Caesar
Feels Like Home – Chantal Kreviazuk
Forever After All – Luke Combs
God Bless the Broken Road – Rascal Flatts
Golden Hour – Kacey Musgraves
Hallelujah – Jeff Buckley
Halo – Beyoncé
Heartbeats – José González
Hold You In My Arms – Ray LaMontagne
How Long Will I Love You – Ellie Goulding
In Case You Didn't Know (Piano Version) - Brett Young
Joy Of My Life– Chris Stapleton
Love Is - Ingrid Michaelson & Jason Mraz
Love Is Alive – Gwen Stefani, Blake Shelton
Love Story – Taylor Swift
Marry Me – Train
Nella Fantasia – Sarah Brightman
Nothing Sweeter - Naomi Sharon
Over The Rainbow – Israel Kamakawiwo'ole
Slow And Steady – Of Monsters And Men
Songbird – Eva Cassidy
Speechless – Dan + Shay
Such Great Heights – Iron And Wine
Sweet Disposition – The Temper Trap
Tenerife Sea – Ed Sheeran
Thank God (Spring Symphony Version) - Kane & Katelyn Brown
The Gift – Jim Brickman, Collin Raye, Susan Ashton
True Companion – Marc Cohn
Wedding Medley – Anthem Lights
Why I Love You – MAJOR.
You Are My Sunshine – Kina Grannis
Yours (Wedding Version) – Russell Dickerson

Classic Romance
Always and Forever – Heatwave
One In A Million – Larry Graham
Ribbon In The Sky – Stevie Wonder
Truly – Lionel Richie
Wedding Song (There Is Love) – Noel Paul Stookey
You and I – Stevie Wonder

New Age Vibe
A Day Without Rain – Enya
Angel Eyes – Jim Brickman
Fairytale – Enya
Hand In Hand – David Arkenstone
Love Story – Luc Serra
May It Be – Enya
Nocturne – Secret Garden
Only Time – Enya
Variations on the Kanon – George Winston

GROOM PROCESSIONAL SONGS

Classic Romance
At Last - Etta James
Here Comes The Sun - Beatles
I Choose You - Willie Hutch
I'm Gonna Make You My Wife - The Whispers
Iris - Goo Goo Dolls
The Chapel Of Love - The Dixie Cups

Modern Romance
All Of Me - John Legend
Beyond – Leon Bridges
Bless the Broken Road – Rascal Flatts
Butterflies – MAX, Ali Gatie
Electric Love – BØRNS
Falling Like The Stars – James Arthur
Find You - Eddie Tom, Tiko Lasola
First Day Of My Life - Bright Eyes
From The Ground Up - Dan + Shay
Her - Isaac Carree
Here I Stand - Usher
Intentions (Acoustic) – Justin Bieber
Joy Of My Life - Chris Stapleton
Let's Get Married - MTV Unplugged - Bleachers
Live Forever – Kane Brown
Look at Me Now – Matt Stell
Marry Me - Train
Marry That Girl - Easton Corbin
Marry Your Daughter - Brian McKnight Jr.
Nobody – Brian McKnight
nobody else – LANY
On My Way To You - Cody Johnson
Prayed For You - Matt Stell
Speechless Acoustic - Dan + Shay
Spend My Life With You - Eric Benet, Kevin "K.D." Davis
The Only One - Music Travel Love
Times Like These (Acoustic) – Foo Fighters
When I Say I Do – Matthew West
When It Comes To You - Fridayy
Wreck - Ben Rector
Yellow - Coldplay
You Are The Reason - Calum Scott

Fun & Upbeat
For Once In My Life - Stevie Wonder
Higher Love – Kygo & Whitney Houston
Let's Get Married - Bleachers
Let's Get Married (ReMarqable Remix) – Jagged Edge
Marry Me - Bruno Mars
Marry Me - Shelley FKA DRAM
Marry Me – Jason Derulo
Men In Black – Will Smith
Missing Piece – Vance Joy
Sharp Dressed Man – ZZ Top
The Man – Aloe Blacc

Instrumentals
10,000 Hours (Piano Version) - Laura Sullivan
Best Day of My Life – Vitamin String Quartet
Here Comes The Sun - Midnight String Quartet
Kiss The Girl - The O'Neill Brothers
Nothing Else Matters (Instrumental Version) – Apocalyptica
Turning PAge Instrumental - Sleeping At Last
Until I Found You - Mike Dawes, Guus Dielissen

Vocal Covers
Better Together – Us The Duo
Can't Help Falling in Love – Music Travel Love
Grow Old With You – Ortopilot
I'm Gonna Be (500 Miles) – Sleeping At Last
Marry You (Acoustic Cover) – The Moon Loungers
Stand By Me – Florence + The Machine
The Book of Love - Gavin James
(What A) Wonderful World - Jonny Brenns
Without You - The Piano Guys

Film & TV
Gonna Fly Now (Rocky Theme) – Bill Conti
Indiana Jones Theme - John Williams
James Bond Theme – The London Symphony Orchestra
Jurassic Park Theme - John Williams
Real American – Rick Derringer
Star Wars Main Theme – John Williams
WWE: I Am Greatness (Roman Reigns) - def rebel

9

Join the Wedding MusicLetter for the latest and trending wedding songs - every Wednesday.

WEDDING PARTY PROCESSIONAL SONGS

Traditional & Elegant
Air On The G String – Johann S Bach
Coronation March – Pyotr Ilyich Tchaikovsky
Gabriel's Oboe – Ennio Morricone
Hand in Hand – David Arkenstone
Highland Cathedral – Royal Scots Dragoon Guards
Pachelbel's Canon in D – Danny Wright
The Prince of Denmark's March – Jeremiah Clarke
Wagner's Bridal Chorus – Keun Young

Classical & New Age Instrumentals
All for You (Instrumental) - The Light the Heat
Better Together (Saxophone Version) - Bobby G
Can't Help Falling in Love – Akiko Meyers, Vieaux
Can't Help Falling In Love – Daniel Jang
Canon in D – Brooklyn Duo
Feels Like Home – Bridesmaids Quartet
Levels - Midnite String Quartet
Nothing Else Matters - Apocalyptica
River Flows in You – Hauser
Something Just Like This - Jennifer Thomas
The Joker And The Queen (Piano Version) – Marlene T
Until I Found You - Paul Hankinson Covers
Wildest Dreams – Dallas String Quartet
Wildest Dreams – Duomo
You Are The Reason – The Piano Guys & DSQ
Young and Beautiful – Ashot Dumanyan

Unique & Non-Traditional
All My Life – Sailr
Anything – JJ Heller
Flower Girl (Wedding Version) - Molly Lovette
I Just Love You (Reimagined for Piano) – Roo Panes
love is just a word – Jasmine Thompson, Calum Scott
loving you – Mahogany Lox
Made to Love You – Drew Angus
Perfect Symphony – Ed Sheeran with Andrea Bocelli
Someone Like Me – Julia Westlin
The First Time – The Brave Collide
When You Love Someone (Live) – Gretchen Peters

Film & TV
A Thousand Years (Twilight) – The Piano Guys
A Thousand Years (Twilight)– Christina Perri
Across the Stars (Star Wars) – John Williams
Disney Medley (Disney) – 40 Fingers
Hold My Hand (Lady Gaga) – Alexandre Pachabezian
I See the Light (Tangled) - Disney Peaceful Strings
Jurassic Park Theme - VSQ
Kiss the Girl (Little Mermaid) - Simon Casey
Married Life (Up) - Michael Giacchino
Marry Me Ballad (Marry Me) – Jennifer Lopez, Maluma
Mercy (Hunger Games) - James Newton Howard
Turning Page Instrumental (Twilight) - Sleeping At Last
Wildest Dreams (Bridgerton) - Duomo
You're the One That I Want (Grease) - Rockoff, Kole

Meant To Be Together
Better Together – Jack Johnson
Bless The Broken Road – Rascal Flatts
Bloom - The Paper Kites
Simply The Best - Noah Reid
The One – Kodaline
this is how you fall in love - Chelsea Cutler, Jeremy Zucker
You Are the Best Thing – Ray LaMontagne

In Love
All Of Me – John Legend
Bright – Echosmith
Can't Help Falling in Love – Kina Grannis
Can't Help Falling In Love – Music Travel Love
Gonna Love You - Parmalee
I Get To Love You – Ruelle
I Love You More – Avery Anna
Imagine (Acoustic) – Ben Platt
In Case You Didn't Know – Brett Young
Love Someone – Lukas Graham
Made for You – Jake Owen
NOTHING NEW (I DO) - Wedding Version - Brandon Lake
So in Love With You – Jonny Houlihan

Getting Married
First Day Of My Life – Bright Eyes
Heavenly Day – Patty Griffin
Marry Me – The Wicks
Marry Me – Tommee Profitt, Fleurie
Marry Me – Train
Marry You - Tayler Holder
No Matter Where You Are (Wedding Version) – Us The Duo
Take My Hand (The Wedding Song) – Hackett, Anderson
Take My Name (Wedding Version) – Parmalee
Today I Do – Tamia
Wedding Medley – Anthem Lights
Wedding Song (Acoustic) – Yeah Yeah Yeahs

Sharing Forever
10,000 Hours (Piano Remix) – Dan + Shay & Justin Bieber
Angel (Acoustic) – Ric Hassani
For a Lifetime - Ryann Darling feat. Cory Ard
Forever – Jaheim
From the Ground Up – Dan + Shay
From This Moment On – Shania Twain, Bryan White
Growing Old With You – Restless Road
I Wanna Grow Old With You - Bride & Groom
I Will Spend My Whole Life Loving You – I. Future & K. Grannis
I'm Yours – Jason Mraz
Lifetime - Justin Bieber
Love You For A Long Time - Maggie Rogers
Never Stop (Wedding Version) – SafetySuit
Over The Rainbow – Israel Kamakawiwo'ole
Unconditionally – Caleb and Kelsey
Yours – Ella Henderson
Yours (Wedding Edition) - Russell Dickerson

Join the Wedding MusicLetter for the latest and trending wedding songs - every Wednesday.

BRIDE PROCESSIONAL SONGS

Modern Instrumental Covers
A Million Dreams - The Piano Guys
A Thousand Years - Daniel Jang
A Thousand Years - The Piano Guys
Accidentally in Love (Wedding Piano Version) - Paul H.
All Of Me - Brooklyn Duo
All Of Me - VioDance
Beauty and the Beast (Piano & Cello) - The Wong Janice
Can't Help Falling In Love (Violin Instrumental) - Alan Ng
El Color de Tus Ojos - Omar Robles, Arcano
Enchanted - Piano Dreamers
Enchanted (The Wedding Violin Version) - Ana Done
From This Moment On - The O'Neill Brothers
Here Comes the Sun (Piano Instrumental) - Benny Martin
I Get To Love You (Instrumental) - Brian Catuccio
I See the Light - Taylor Davis
Joy of My Life (Instrumental) - Guitar Tribute Players
Love Me Like You Do (Cinematic Version) - VioDance
Nothing Else Matters (Instrumental Version) - VioDance
She Will Be Loved - Guitar Tribute Players
Something in the Orange (Instrumental) - Philip Bowen
The Princess Bride - Storybook Love - VSQ
To Make You Feel My Love - The O'Neill Brothers
Turning Page (Instrumental) - Sleeping At Last
Wedding Entrance X Can't Help Falling In Love - J. Wong
Wildest Dreams - Duomo
Yellow - Brooklyn Duo

Traditional & Elegant
Bridal Chorus - Richard Wagner
Canon in D - Brooklyn Duo
Canon in D - Johann Pachelbel
Flower of Scotland - The Royal Scots Dragoon Guard
Wedding March - Felix Mendelssohn

Romantic Vocal Covers
Can't Help Falling in Love - Haley Reinhart
Can't Help Falling in Love - Kacey Musgraves
Can't Help Falling In Love - Kina Grannis
Fields Of Gold - Eva Cassidy
First Date (Acoustic) - Taylor Acorn
I'm Gonna Be (500 Miles) - Sleeping At Last
Iris - Kina Grannis
Simply The Best - Billianne
Stand By Me - Florence + The Machine

Original Instrumentals
Across the Stars - John Williams
Concerning Hobbits - Howard Shore
Kiss the Rain - Yiruma
Main Theme From Jurassic Park - John Williams
Married Life - Michael Giacchino

Joy & Excitement
Just The Way You Are - Bruno Mars
Marry Me - Shelley FKA DRAM
Marry Me - Train
Marry You - Bruno Mars

Romantic Love
A Thousand Years - Christina Perri
All Of Me - John Legend
Beautiful Crazy (Acoustic) - Luke Combs
Biblical - Calum Scott
Bloom - The Paper Kites
Enchanted - Taylor Swift
First Day Of My Life - Bright Eyes
Giving Myself - Jennifer Hudson
Grow Old With You - Ortopilot
I Choose You - Amanda Jordan
I Get To Love You - Ruelle
I'm Gonna Love You - Jessie James Decker
If You Love Her - Forest Blakk feat. Meghan Trainor
Joy Of My Life - Chris Stapleton
Lifetime - Justin Bieber
Look at Me - Carrie Underwood
Looking For You - Fantasia feat. Mama Diane
Love Me Like You Do (Acoustic) - Ellie Goulding
Lover - Taylor Swift
Make You Feel My Love - Adele
My Song - H.E.R.
Never Til Now - Ashley Cooke
NOTHING NEW (I DO) [Wedding Version] - Brandon Lake
Over The Rainbow - Israel Kamakawiwo'ole
Perfect - Ed Sheeran
Promise to Love Her - Blane Howard
Speechless (Acoustic) - Dan + Shay
Stargazing (Moonlight Version) - Myles Smith
That's What Love Is - Alexandra Kay
This Is It - Scotty McCreery
Tuesdays - Jake Scott
When I See You - Aaron Watson
You Are The Reason - Calum Scott

Classic Romance
At Last - Etta James
Can't Help Falling In Love - Elvis Presley
Here Comes The Sun - Beatles
I Don't Want to Miss a Thing - Aerosmith
In My Life - Beatles
Love Of My Life - Queen
Songbird - Fleetwood Mac

Unique & Non-Traditional
Flower Girl - Molly Lovette
I'm Sure It's You (The Wedding Song) - Sheléa
If You Love Her (Acoustic) - Forest Blakk
Life at First Sight - Alexander Stewart
Lucky Me - Jake Miller
My Feet Don't Touch the Ground - Bonner Rhae
Patience - Madilyn Paige
Runnin' Home to You - Grant Gustin
The One My Heart Beats For - Greg Steinfeld
Walk in a Room (Reimagined) – Muscadine Bloodline
You Set My World On Fire - Loving Caliber

Join the Wedding MusicLetter for the latest and trending wedding songs - every Wednesday.

UNITY CEREMONY SONGS

Instrumental Elegance
Air on a G String - Hauser
All Of Me – Daniel Jang
Canon in D - Brooklyn Duo
Compass (Cinematic Version) – Analog Heart
Hand in Hand - David Arkenstone
Hand in Hand - Thad Fiscella
Infinity (Piano Version) - Flying Fingers
Just the Way You Are – The Piano Guys
Love One Another - Paul Cardall
Make You Feel My Love – Casper Esmann
One Hand, One Heart – O'Neill Brothers Group

Forever Love
A Thousand Years – Christina Perri
Always and Forever – Heatwave
By My Side – Ben Harper
Faithfully – Brian McKnight
For a Lifetime – Ryann Darling feat. Cory Ard
For Life - Moses Bliss
Forever From Now – Sheffield
From This Moment On – Shania Twain & Bryan White
Happily Ever After – Case
I Am Yours – Andy Grammer
I Could Never Love You Enough – Brian McComas
I Get to Love You – Ruelle
I Will Spend My Whole Life Loving You – Future & Grannis
If I Didn't Love You - Ben Abraham
If It Were Up To Me – Johnny and Heidi
Inseparable – Natalie Cole
Last Love - Jon Mullins
Never Stop (Wedding Version) – SafetySuit
Our Forever - Spencer Crandall
Touching Heaven – JOHNNYSWIM
Wherever Time Goes – Jake & Brittney Hoot
Worth It – Ryan Cabrera
Yours – Ella Henderson
Yours – Russell Dickerson

Modern Romance
All Because of You – O.A.R.
All You Need Is Love – Katy Perry
Could I Love You Any More – R. Dominique, J. Mraz
Fall for You – Leela James
Greatest Love Story – LANCo
Guiding Light – Foy Vance feat. Ed Sheeran
Love Someone – Lukas Graham
Make You Feel My Love – Blessing Offor, Bob Lanzetti
Sent From Heaven – Rahsaan Patterson
Songbird – Rita Wilson, Josh Groban
The One – Kodaline
When You Love Someone (MTV Unplugged) – Bryan Adams
When You Say Nothing At All – Music Travel Love

Celebrating Unity
All Your'n – Tyler Childers
Better Half – JJ Heller
Breathe - Caleb and Kelsey
Here, Right Now – Joshua Radin
I Belong to You – Jacob Lee
I Choose You (Acoustic) – Kiana Ledé
I Do – Monique Melendez, Byron Addison
I Found A Love (Live at Levon Helm Studios) – J. James, Taa
I Would, I Could, I Do (Duet) - Treela
Marry Me – Martina McBride and Pat Monahan
Nothing Lost – The Alternate Routes
One + One - Lawson Bates, Olivia Collingsworth
One Flame – Amber Norgaard
Ritual – Chadwick Johnson
Sing Me a Song – William Prince, Serena Ryder
Stumble Together - Matt Bednarsky
Take My Hand (The Wedding Song) - Hackett, Anderson
The Wedding Song – Matthew Mole
Today I Do – Tamia
Two Becoming One – Jonathan and Emily Martin
Wedding Song (There Is Love) – Noel Paul Stookey
When I Said I Do – Clint Black and Lisa Hartman Black
When You Married Me – Andrew Brien
Your Hands - Mae Estes

Making a Promise
All My Life – SAILR
Always Be Yours - Scott Drury
Chance of a Lifetime (The Proposal) - Cory Singer
For You – Kenny Lattimore
Giving It All (To You) – Haley & Michaels
Hold Us Tight (Acoustic) – The Macarons Project
I Choose You – Sara Bareilles
I Chose You – Caleb Edens
I Do – Casi Joy
I've Made Up My Mind to Give Myself to You – Bob Dylan
Lover of Mine - Louyah
Make You Mine – Meg Ammons
My Word – Derran Day
No Matter Where You Are (Wedding Version) - Us The Duo
Promise To Love Her – Blane Howard
Promise You That - Trevor Martin
When I Say I Do – Matthew West

Religious
A Page Is Turned – Bebo Norman
Amazing Grace – Lari White
Ave Maria – Beyonce
Ave Maria – Luciano Pavarotti
Believe in Love – Charlie Worsham
Faithful Friend – Twila Paris & Steven Curtis Chapman
Flesh Of My Flesh – Leon Patillo
Hallelujah – Alison Sparrow
The Prayer – Celine Dion, Andrea Bocelli

Join the Wedding MusicLetter for the latest and trending wedding songs - every Wednesday.

MEMORIAL SONGS

Father/Dad/Papa
Dance With My Father - Luther Vandross
Heaven Right Now - Thomas Rhett
If You Could See Me Now - The Script
Jealous of the Angels - Jenn Bostic
Monsters - James Blunt
My Old Man - Zac Brown Band
Remember Him That Way - Luke Combs
Song For Dad - Keith Urban
Thank You for Being My Dad - Jon Barker
The Living Years - Mike + The Mechanics
When I Get There - Pink
You Should Be Here - Cole Swindell

Mother/Mom/Mama
Bye Mom - Chris Janson
Dance - NAS
Goodnight, Travel Well - The Killers
Heaven's Not Too Far - We Three
Love You Forever - G-Eazy
Mother - Sleeping At Last
One More I Love You - Alex Warren
Supermarket Flowers - Ed Sheeran
Two Of Us - Louis Tomlinson

Grandma/Mom Mom
Holes In The Floor Of Heaven - Steve Wariner

Grandpa/Pop Pop
Million Miles - Angelina Jordan
When I Get Where I'm Going - B. Paisley, D. Parton

Child
Angels In Waiting - Tammy Cochran
Heaven Bound Balloons - Granger Smith
Liam's Song - Tainted Lyric
Tears in Heaven - Eric Clapton
The Father, My Son, and the Holy Ghost - Craig Morgan
Who'd You Be Today - Kenny Chesney

Military Person
Arlington - Trace Adkins
If Heaven Was Needing A Hero - Jo Dee Messina
Some Gave All - Billy Ray Cyrus
The Ones Who Didn't Make it Back Home - Justin Moore
Travelin' Soldier - The Chicks

Having an Angel
Angel Standing - Jewel
Angels - Robbie Williams
Angels Among Us - Alabama
For Always - Josh Groban
I'll Be There - Escape Club
When I Look To The Sky - Train

Sibling/Friend
100% - Sonic Youth
Afterimage - Rush
An Original Man (A Song for Keith) - Yardbirds
Beat You There - Will Dempsey
Being Boring - Pet Shop Boys
Broken Halos - Chris Stapleton
Cryin' For Me (Wayman's Song) - Toby Keith
Drink A Beer - Luke Bryan
Drowning - Chris Young
F64 - Ed Sheeran
Gone Too Soon - Michael Jackson
Heaven Right Now - Thomas Rhett
I'll Be Missing You - Puff Daddy & Faith Evans
In Loving Memory - Alter Bridge
Missing You - Diana Ross
One Tree Hill - U2
People Are Crazy - Billy Currington
See You Again - Wiz Khalifa feat. Charlie Puth
Show Me Around - Carly Pearce
So Far Away - Avenged Sevenfold
Tha Crossroads - Bone Thugs-N-Harmony
The Last Song - Foo Fighters
Wish You Were Here - Bee Gees

Someone Special
21 Days - Brian Fallon
Bigger Than The Whole Sky - Taylor Swift
Coming Back Down - Hollywood Undead
Dancing in the Sky - Dani and Lizzy
Eyes Closed - Ed Sheeran
Forever Loving You - Tanya Tucker
Gone Too Soon - Simple Plan
I Will Remember You - Sarah McLachlan
If Heaven Had a Landline - Brian Congdon
It's So Hard To Say Goodbye To Yesterday - Boyz II Men
Knowing You - Kenny Chesney
Lay Me Down - Sam Smith
Let Somebody Go - Coldplay X Selena Gomez
Life In A Northern Town - Dream Academy
Lifetime - Three Days Grace
Lift Me Up - Rihanna
My Heart Will Go On - Celine Dion
Never Not Remember You - Cooper Alan
Red Bird - HunterGirl
Sad Song - We The Kings, Elena Coats
Show Me Around - Carly Pearce
Visiting Hours - Ed Sheeran
With Me - Sum 41

Recent Passing
Bye Bye - Mariah Carey
Go Rest High on That Mountain - Vince Gill
Liquor Store In The Sky - BJ The Chicago Kid
Time To Say Goodbye (Con Te Partiro) - Sarah Brightman

Join the Wedding MusicLetter for the latest and trending wedding songs - every Wednesday.

RECESSIONAL SONGS

Upbeat
A Sky Full Of Stars - Coldplay
Accidentally In Love - Counting Crows
Ain't No Mountain High Enough - Jennifer Hudson
All You Need Is Love - Katy Perry
Always Be My Baby - Brasstracks
Beautiful Day - U2
Belong Together - Mark Amber
Beside You - James Blunt
Best Day Of My Life - American Authors
Better - Khalid
Brand New - Ben Rector
Carry You Home - Alex Warren
Come and Get Your Love - Redbone
Crazy Little Thing Called Love - Queen
Dreaming - Marshmello, P!NK, Sting
Electric Love - Børns
Everywhere - Fleetwood Mac
Fly Me To The Moon - Frank Sinatra
Forever - Chris Brown
Forever And For Always - Shania Twain
Good Day - Forrest Frank
Good Life - Onerepublic
Home - Edward Sharpe & The Magnetic Zeros
How Sweet It Is (To Be Loved By You) - James Taylor
I Do - Colbie Caillat
I'm A Believer - Smash Mouth
I'm In Love With You - The 1975
If I Didn't Have You - BANNERS
Love On Top - Beyonce
Lovely Day - Bill Withers
Marry Me - Jason Derulo
Miracles Happen (When You Believe) - Myra
Now That We Found Love - Heavy D. & the Boyz
On Top Of The World - Imagine Dragons
Paper Rings - Taylor Swift
Rather Be - Clean Bandit, Jess Glynne
Rest of Our Lives - The Light the Heat
Run Away With Me - Cold War Kids
Say Hey (I Love You) - Michael Franti & Spearhead
September - Earth Wind & Fire
Signed, Sealed, Delivered, I'm Yours - Stevie Wonder
Smile - Martin Garrix feat. Carolina Liar
Stuck Like Glue - Sugarland
This Will Be (An Everlasting Love) - Natalie Cole
We Found Love - Rihanna, Calvin Harris
What Dreams Are Made Of - Hilary Duff
Would You Go With Me - Josh Turner
You & I - Rita Ora
You Are The Best Thing - Ray LaMontagne
You Make My Dreams Come True - Hall & Oates
(Your Love Keeps Lifting Me) Higher & Higher - J. Wilson

Classic Romance
At Last - Etta James
Here Comes The Sun - The Beatles
Nothing's Gonna Stop Us Now - Starship
Over The Rainbow - Israel Kamakawiwo'ole
What A Wonderful World - Louis Armstrong
What Are You Doing The Rest Of Your Life? - Chris Botti, Sting
Modern Romance
10,000 Hours (Piano Remix) - Dan + Shay, Justin Bieber
A Thousand Years - Christina Perri
All My Life - Sailr
All Your'n - Tyler Childers
Better Together - Jack Johnson
Bittersweet Symphony - The Verve
Can't Help Falling in Love - Kina Grannis
Carry Me Away - John Mayer
Cowboy Take Me Away - The Chicks
Evermore - Hollow Coves
Finally Mine - Juliet Roberts
First Day Of My Life - Bright Eyes
For a Lifetime - Ryann Darling, Cory Ard
Forever From Now - Sheffield
Grow As We Go - Ben Platt
Grow Old - Florida Georgia Line
Higher Love - James Vincent McMorrow
I Am Yours - Andy Grammer
I Get to Love You - Ruelle
Keep Her - Johnny and Heidi
Love Me Like You Do - Ellie Goulding
Made for You - Jake Owen
Marry Me - Train
My Love Will Follow You - Dave Barnes
Take My Name - Parmalee
Thank God - Kane Brown, Katelyn Brown
This Is It - Scotty McCreery
We Are Man And Wife - Michelle Featherstone
Yours - Ella Henderson
Traditional & Elegant
Canon in D - Brooklyn Duo
Hand in Hand - David Arkenstone
Highland Cathedral - Royal Scots Dragoon Guards
River Flows in You - Hauser
Trumpet Tune - Henry Purcell
Wildest Dreams - Duomo
Acoustic
Brand New Day (Acoustic 2020) - Joshua Radin
Forever And Ever, Amen - Ronan Keating, Shania Twain
I Don't Want to Miss a Thing - Music Travel Love
No Matter Where You Are (Wedding Version) - Us The Duo
Ocean - LunchMoney Lewis, Meghan Trainor
Yours (Wedding Edition) - Russell Dickerson

COCKTAIL HOUR SONGS

Rat Pack
A Kiss To Build A Dream On – Louis Armstrong
A Sunday Kind Of Love – Etta James
All Of You – Sammy Davis Jr.
Everybody Loves Somebody – Dean Martin
Feeling Good – Michael Buble
Fly Me To The Moon – Frank Sinatra, Count Basie
Hallelujah, I Love Her So – Ray Charles
It's Not Unusual – Tom Jones
L-O-V-E – Nat King Cole
Mack The Knife – Bobby Darin

Motown
Baby, I Love You – Aretha Franklin
Be My Baby – The Ronettes
Being With You – Smokey Robinson
I'll Be Around – The Spinners
Never Too Much – Luther Vandross
Nightshift – Commodores
Rock With You – Michael Jackson
Something's Got A Hold On Me – Etta James
Stand By Me – Otis Redding
You're A Wonderful One – Marvin Gaye

Yacht Rock
Biggest Part Of Me – Ambrosia
Caribbean Queen – Billy Ocean
Do It Again – Steely Dan
Human Nature – Michael Jackson
Listen To The Music – The Doobie Brothers
Love Will Keep Us Together – Captain & Tennille
Lovely Day – Bill Withers
Sailing – Christopher Cross
We're In This Love Together – Al Jarreau
You Can Do Magic – America

Acoustic
Beautiful Soul – Boyce Avenue
Better Together – Us The Duo
Can't Help Falling In Love – Kina Grannis
Grow Old With You – ortoPilot
Make You Feel My Love – Shane Filan
Meant To Be Acoustic – Bebe Rexha
Simply The Best – The Moon Loungers
Watermelon Sugar – Jonah Baker
Yellow – Penny Sweet
You Are My Sunshine – Music Travel Love

Sing-alongs
A Thousand Miles – Vanessa Carlton
Ain't No Mountain High Enough – Jennifer Hudson
Angel – Shaggy, Rayvon
I Want It That Way – Backstreet Boys
I'm A Believer – Smash Mouth
Just The Way You Are – Bruno Mars
Love On Top – Beyonce
Roar – Katy Perry
You Belong With Me (Taylor's Version) – Taylor Swift

Modern R&B
4 Me – Don Toliver, Kali Uchis
After Hours – Kehlani
Baby Will You Love Me – MAJOR.
Be The One – Bree Runway & Khalid
HERicane – Lucky Daye
Keeps On Fallin' – Babyface, Ella Mai
Me & U – Tems
Smooth Sailin' – Leon Bridges
Your Love Is All I Need – Vedo
your love is life – Musiq Soulchild, Hit-Boy

Modern Hip Hop
All the Stars – Kendrick Lamar & SZA
Cinderella – Future, Metro Boomin, Travis Scott
Creepin' – Metro Boomin, The Weeknd, 21 Savage
First Class – Jack Harlow
I Like You (A Happier Song) – Post Malone, Doja Cat
I'm the One – DJ Khaled
marry me – KANII
Paint The Town Red – Doja Cat
Sunflower – Post Malone, Swae Lee
What It Is (Solo Version) – Doechii

Modern Country
Buy Dirt – Jordan Davis, Luke Bryan
Dancin' In The Moonlight – Chris Lane, Lauren Alaina
Falling For You – Niko Moon
Fooled Around and Fell in Love – Miranda Lambert & Friends
Happy Anywhere – Blake Shelton, Gwen Stefani
Just the Way – Parmalee & Blanco Brown
Pour Me A Drink – Post Malone, Blake Shelton
Steal My Love – Dan + Shay
The Painter – Cody Johnson
Whatever Forever Is – Devin Dawson

Modern Indie Rock
All 4 Nothing (I'm So In Love) – Lauv
Birds of a Feather – Billie Eilish
Good Together – Lake Street Dive
I'm In Love With You – The 1975
Lost In Space – Foster The People
Missing Piece – Vance Joy
Pineapple Sunrise – Beach Weather
Stargazing – Myles Smith
Tiny Moves – Bleachers
Whatever – Walk Off the Earth

Tropical House
Bloom – Lucas Estrada, TWOPILOTS
Fast Car – Jonas Blue, Dakota
Lifetime – SG Lewis
Little Bit More – Suriel Hess
Stumblin' In – CYRIL
Sway My Way – R3HAB, Amy Shark
Time After Time – Paratone
Walking On Sunshine – CARSTN, Katrina & the Waves
What A Wonderful World – SOFI TUKKER

Join the Wedding MusicLetter for the latest and trending wedding songs - every Wednesday.

ENTRANCE & INTRO SONGS

Classy Entrance
All You Need Is Love – The Beatles
Best Day Of My Life – American Authors
Classic – MKTO
Come And Get Your Love – Redbone
Fly Me To The Moon – Imaginary Future
Gimme! Gimme! Gimme! (A Man After Midnight) - ABBA
How Sweet It Is (To Be Loved By You) – James Taylor
Music For a Sushi Restaurant - Harry Styles

Romantic
A Guy with a Girl – Blake Shelton
All To Myself – Dan + Shay
Beautiful In White – Shane Filan
Beyond – Leon Bridges
Marry Me – Train
Say Hey (I Love You) – Michael Franti & Spearhead

TV & Film
Eye Of The Tiger – Survivor
Game Of Thrones Theme – Ramin Djawadi
Gonna Fly Now (Rocky Theme) – Bill Conti
James Bond Theme – Royal Philharmonic Orchestra
Jurassic Park (Main Theme) – John Williams
Star Wars (Main Theme) – Meco
Top Gun Anthem – H. Faltermeyer & S. Stevens

We Were Meant To Be
Brand New – Ben Rector
Crazy In Love – Beyonce
Electric Love - BØRNS
Forever – Chris Brown
Good Life – OneRepublic
Good To Be Alive (Hallelujah) – Andy Grammer
Home – Edward Sharpe & The Magnetic Zeros
I'll Be There For You – The Rembrandts
L'amour Toujours – Gigi D'Agostino
Lighter - Galantis, David Guetta, 5 Seconds Of Summer
Love On Top – Beyonce
Stuck Like Glue – Sugarland
Walking On Sunshine – Katrina & The Waves
We Are One - 3 Are Legend, Bryn Christopher
We Found Love – Rihanna ft. Calvin Harris
You Make My Dreams – Daryl Hall & John Oates

We Made It
Down – Jay Sean feat. Lil Wayne
From This Moment On – Shania Twain, Bryan White
Let's Get Married (ReMarqable Remix) – Jagged Edge
Marry You – Bruno Mars
Movie Star - Steve Aoki, MOD SUN, Global Dan
On Top Of The World – Imagine Dragons
Setting the World on Fire – Kenny Chesney with P!nk
Signed, Sealed, Delivered, I'm Yours – Stevie Wonder
This Will Be (An Everlasting Love) - Natalie Cole

We Will Survive
Cheerleader – OMI
Feel So Close – Calvin Harris
I Believe In A Thing Called Love – Darkness
Iconic - Simple Plan
Stand by You – Rachel Patten
The Only Way Is Up - Apoc
Tubthumping – Chumbawamba
What A Night - Flo Rida

Tonight Is Our Night
24k Magic – Bruno Mars
A Sky Full of Stars – Coldplay
Amazing – Mary J. Blige feat. DJ Khaled
Beautiful Day – U2
Born For This – The Score
Bring 'Em Out – T.I. Feat. Jay-Z
Can't Hold Us – Macklemore & Ryan Lewis feat. Ray Dalton
Everybody (Backstreet's Back) – Backstreet Boys
Glorious – UNSECRET
Moment 4 Life – Nicki Minaj
My House – Flo Rida
Now That We Found Love – Heavy D. & The Boyz
September – Earth, Wind & Fire
Welcome To My House - Yonaka Rock
Welcome to the Party – Diplo, French Montana

Get Hyped
100 Lives - Jonas Blue & Eyelar
All I Do Is Win – DJ Khaled
Can't Stop The Feeling! – Justin Timberlake
Celebration - Kool & The Gang
Clap Your Hands - Oh the Larceny
Crowd Go Crazy – John Legend
Dance The Night - Dua Lipa
Dynamite – Taio Cruz
Get Ready For This – 2 Unlimited
Get The Party Started – P!nk
Handclap – Fitz & The Tantrums
I Feel Good – Pitbull
I Gotta Feeling – Black Eyed Peas
I'm Good (Blue) - David Guetta, Bebe Rexha
Let's Get It Started – Black Eyed Peas
Let's Get Loud - Jennifer Lopez
Let's Go Crazy - Prince
Levels – Avicii
One More Time - Daft Punk
Party Rock Anthem – LMFAO
Raise Your Glass - P!nk
Run Free (Countdown) - Tiësto & R3HAB
Shut Up And Dance – Walk The Moon
Thunderstruck – AC/DC
Turn Down For What – DJ Snake feat. Lil Jon
Uptown Funk – Mark Ronson feat. Bruno Mars
We Will Rock You – Queen
Yeah! – Usher feat. Lil Jon and Ludacris

FIRST DANCE SONGS

Modern Romance
All of Me - John Legend & Lindsey Stirling
All the Way - Shane Smith & the Saints
All Your'n - Tyler Childers
Amazing – Teddy Swims
Amen – John Adams
Baby I'm Yours - Artic Monkeys
Beautiful Crazy – Luke Combs
Better Together - Luke Combs
Beyond – Leon Bridges
Conversations In The Dark - John Legend
Dance With You - Brett Young
Find Someone Like You – Snoh Aalegra
First Date (Acoustic) – Taylor Acorn
Forever After All – Luke Combs
From The Ground Up - Dan + Shay
I Am Yours – Andy Grammer
In Case You Didn't Know – Brett Young
In Your Love – Tyler Childers
Joy of My Life – Chris Stapleton
Life With You - Kelsey Hart
Lifetime – Justin Bieber
Love Someone – Lukas Graham
Love You Anyway – Devon Gilfillian
Love You Anyway – Luke Combs
Lover - Taylor Swift
Made For Me – Muni Long
Made to Love You – Drew Angus
My Best Friend - Tim McGraw
My Person (Wedding Version) – Spencer Crandall
Never Stop (Wedding Version) – SafetySuit
Perfect - Ed Sheeran
Perfect For Me – Bradley Marshall
Pointless – Lewis Capaldi
Promise to Love Her – Blane Howard
Say You Won't Let Go – James Arthur
Sent From Heaven – Rahsaan Patterson
Tennessee Whiskey - Chris Stapleton
That's What Love Is – Alexandra Kay
Until I Found You - Stephen Sanchez
You (Acoustic) – Dan + Shay

New
10-90 - Muscadine Bloodline
All I Want Is You - The Decemberists
Forever - Noah Kahan
Forever To Me - Cole Swindell
Let's Fall In Love - Raheem DeVaughn
Lost in You (Remix) - Jade Novah & Kevin Ross

Classic Romance
Amazed - Lonestar
At Last - Etta James
Bless the Broken Road - Rascal Flatts
Can't Help Falling In Love - Elvis Presley
Can't Take My Eyes Off Of You - Frankie Valli
Everything – Mary J. Blige
I Cross My Heart - George Strait
I Don't Want To Miss A Thing - Aerosmith
Stand By Me - Ben E. King
The Way You Look Tonight - Frank Sinatra
Wonderful Tonight - Eric Clapton

Duets
Anything For You (The Duet) – Ledisi & PJ Morton
Best Part – H.E.R. feat. Daniel Caesar
If You Love Her – Forest Blakk feat. Meghan Trainor
Like I'm Gonna Lose You – Meghan Trainor feat. John Legend
Never Til Now – Ashley Cooke, Brett Young
Nobody But You – Blake Shelton, Gwen Stefani
Space In My Heart - Enrique Iglesias, Miranda Lambert
Thank God - Kane Brown & Katelyn Brown
The Rest of Our Life – Tim McGraw & Faith Hill
You Are The Reason – Calum Scott & Leona Lewis

LGBTQ+
Biblical - Calum Scott
Heaven – Calum Scott
Imagine (Acoustic) – Ben Platt
Sweet Symphony – Joy Oladokun, Chris Stapleton

Movies & Film
A Thousand Years - Christina Perri (Twilight)
I'll Never Love Again - Lady Gaga (A Star Is Born)

Unique
Best Friend - Pacific Skyway
Dressed Up In White - Cal
Evermore – Hollow Coves
Forever From Now – Sheffield
I GUESS I'M IN LOVE – Clinton Kane
I Will Spend My Whole Life Loving You – I. Future & K. Grannis
If I Didn't Love You – Ben Abraham
Luckiest Man – Clark Beckham

Upbeat and Fun
Dancing Queen - ABBA
I Wanna Dance With Somebody - Whitney Houston
September - Earth, Wind & Fire
Shut Up and Dance - Walk the Moon
You Are The Best Thing – Ray Lamontagne

Written for a Dance
Always Gonna Love You (First Dance Version) – Alana Springsteen
First Dance - Hasan Green
First Dancin' - 2 Lane Summer
Growing Old With You (First Dance Version) – Restless Road
Lover (First Dance Remix) – Taylor Swift
Spin You Around (1/24) - Morgan Wallen

Join the Wedding MusicLetter for the latest and trending wedding songs - every Wednesday.

DINNER MUSIC

Bossa Nova Jazz
A Night To Remember – beabadoobee, Laufey
Africa – Deuce
Baby, I Love Your Way – Michelle Simonal
From The Start – Laufey
More Than Words – Groove Da Praia
Rocket Man – Laza Bossa
Say You Won't Let Go – Pablo Cepeda
Soul Bossa Nova – Grace Kelly feat. Sean Jones
Stand By Me – Sarah Menescal
Unwritten – Dinah York

Modern Classical
Chasing Cars – Simply Three
Diamonds – Hannah V, Joe Rodwell
Halo – Caleb Chan, Brian Chan
Higher Love – Music Lab Collective
If I Ain't Got You – Vitamin String Quartet
Love Me Like You Do – Brooklyn Duo
Riptide – Duomo
We Found Love – 2Cellos
Wildest Dreams – Duomo
Wrecking Ball – Midnite String Quartet

Modern Country
All On Me – Devin Dawson
Are You Gonna Kiss Me Or Not – Thompson Square
Blessed – Thomas Rhett
Bluebird – Miranda Lambert
Family Table – Zac Brown Band
GOOD TIME – Niko Moon
Meant to Be – Bebe Rexha, Florida Georgia Line
Play It Again – Luke Bryan
Rumor – Lee Brice
Yeah Boy – Kelsea Ballerini

Modern Folk
Alone With You – Canyon City
Flowers In Your Hair – The Lumineers
Give Me One Reason – Tracy Chapman
I Was Born To Love You – R. LaMontagne, S. Ferrell
My Silver Lining – First Aid Kit
Rest of Our Lives – The Light the Heat
September Song (Guitar Acoustic) – JP Cooper
Simply The Best – Billianne
The Night We Met – Lord Huron
Where's My Love – SYML

Yacht Rock
Aja – Steely Dan
Biggest Part Of Me – Ambrosia
Escape (The Pina Colada Song) – Rupert Holmes
Georgy Porgie – Toto
Kiss On My List – Daryl Hall & John Oates
Listen To The Music – The Doobie Brothers
Lowdown – Boz Scaggs
Sailing – Christopher Cross
This Is It – Kenny Loggins

Modern Pop
Always Be My Baby – Mariah Carey
Calm Down – Rema & Selena Gomez
feelslikeimfallinginlove - Coldplay
Fresh Eyes – Andy Grammer
I Want It That Way – Backstreet Boys
Love On The Brain – Rihanna
Marvin Gaye – Charlie Puth, Meghan Trainor
Put Your Records On – Corinne Bailey Rae
Sunflower – Post Malone & Swae Lee
This Town – Niall Horan

R&B Soul
Ain't Nothin Like The One I've Got – Calvin Richardson
Can't Get Enough Of Your Love, Babe – Jason Morales
Coming Home – Leon Bridges
Drift Away – Jac Ross
How Deep Is Your Love – PJ Morton
In Your Eyes (Remix) – The Weeknd, Kenny G
IT'S YOU – MAX, keshi
Leave The Door Open – Silk Sonic
Smile – Otis Kane
This Is – Ella Mai

Rat Pack
Fly Me To The Moon – Frank Sinatra & Count Basie
I Get A Kick Out Of You – Tony Bennett & Lady Gaga
It Had To Be You – Harry Connick Jr.
It's Not Unusual – Tom Jones
More – Bobby Darin
Sway – Michael Bublé
That's Amore – Dean Martin
The Coffee Song – Frank Sinatra
Valerie (BBC Radio 1 Live Lounge) – Amy Winehouse

Tropical House
Dancing In The Moonlight – Braeten
Everywhere – Toby Rose, Zita
Fast Car – Jonas Blue – Dakota
Just The Two of Us – Yuann Miller
My Girl – Shoby & SHM
Riptide – TWOPILOTS
Stumblin' In – CYRIL
Time After Time – Paratone
What A Wonderful World – Sofi Tukker
Woke Up in Love (Acoustic) – Kygo, Gryffin, Calum Scott

Vocal Acoustic Covers
Can't Help Falling In Love – Kina Grannis
Cheerleader – Pentatonix
Nothing Compares 2 U – Chris Cornell
Stand By Me (Acoustic) – Matt Johnson
Stay With Me – Hannah Trigwell
Stuck on You – Dave Fenley
Watermelon Sugar (Acoustic) – Jonah Baker
When You Say Nothing at All – Music Travel Love
You're Still The One – Teddy Swims
You're the One That I Want – D. Rockoff, C. Kole

CAKE CUTTING SONGS

Classic Love Songs
All My Life – K-Ci & JoJo
At Last – Etta James
Can't Help Falling In Love – Elvis Presley
Can't Take My Eyes Off Of You – Frankie Valli
From This Moment On – Shania Twain
My Best Friend – Tim McGraw
Shower Me With Your Love – Surface
Stand By Me – Ben. E. King
What A Wonderful World – Louis Armstrong

Modern Love Songs
A Moment Like This – Kelly Clarkson
A Thousand Years – Christina Perri
All Of Me – John Legend
Better Together – Jack Johnson
Every Kind Of Way – H.E.R.
Find Someone Like You – Snoh Aalegra
Forever After All – Luke Combs
Perfect – Ed Sheeran
Thank God – Katelyn Brown, Kane Brown
Thinking Out Loud – Ed Sheeran
Why I Love You – MAJOR.
Wonderful – Arika Kane feat. Kmelz
You (Acoustic) – Dan + Shay

Upbeat Love Songs
Beautiful Day – U2
Best Day Of My Life – American Authors
Everything – Michael Buble
Good Life – OneRepublic
Greatest Love Story – LANCo
Home – Edward Sharpe & The Magnetic Zeros
Honey Bee – Blake Shelton
I Do – Colbie Caillat
ily (i love you baby) – Surf Mesa
Just The Way You Are – Bruno Mars
L-O-V-E – Nat King Cole
Love On Top – Beyonce
Love Somebody – Rotimi
Marry Me – Train
Say Hey (I Love You) – Michael Franti & Spearhead
Stuck Like Glue – Sugarland
This Will Be (An Everlasting Love) – Natalie Cole
You Are The Best Thing – Ray Lamontagne

First Dance Remixes
Amazing Strings Version – Teddy Swims
Another Wedding Version – Adam Doleac
First Date Acoustic – Taylor Acorn
Growing Old With You First Dance Version – Restless Road
Lover (Remix) – Tylor Swift, Shawn Mendes
Take My Name Wedding Version – Parmalee
Woke Up In Love Acoustic – Kygo, Gryffin, Calum Scott

Fun Throwbacks
Ain't No Mountain High Enough – M. Gaye and T. Terrell
All You Need Is Love – The Beatles
Because of You – Ne-Yo
Better Be Good To Me – Tina Turner
Chapel Of Love – The Dixie Cups
Come and Get Your Love – Redbone
Fly Me To The Moon (In Other Words) – F. Sinatra & C. Basie
Just The Two of Us – Grover Washington Jr., Bill Withers
Lean On Me – Bill Withers
Love and Marriage – Frank Sinatra
Signed, Sealed, Delivered I'm Yours – Stevie Wonder
That's Amore – Dean Martin
You Make My Dreams – Hall & Oates

Cake Theme
Birthday Cake – Rihanna
Cake – Flo Rida & 99 Percent
Cake & Candy – Rupaul
Cake By The Ocean – DNCE
Casi Casi – Anitta
Cut It – O.T. Genasis, Young Dolph
Cut The Cake – Average White Band
Love You Madly – Cake
Wedding Cake – dvsn, Ty Dolla $ign
Yummy – Justin Bieber
Yummy Yummy Yummy – Ohio Express

Sugar Theme
Pour Some Sugar On Me – Def Leppard
Suga Suga – Baby Bash, Frankie J
Sugar – Maroon 5
Sugar – Surf Curse
Sugar, Sugar – The Archies
Sugar, You – Oh Honey
Watermelon Sugar – Harry Styles

Dessert Theme
Candyman – Christina Aguilera
Cups and Cakes – Spinal Tap
I Can't Help Myself (Sugar Pie, Honey Bunch) – Four Tops
I Want Candy – Bow Wow Wow
Ice Cream – BLACKPINK with Selena Gomez
Ice Cream – Sarah McLachlan
Lollipop – The Chordettes

Sweet Theme
How Sweet It Is – Michael Buble
How Sweet It Is (To Be Loved By You) – James Taylor
Make It Sweet – Old Dominion
Sweet Emotion – Aerosmith
Sweet Thing – Keith Urban
The Sweet Escape – Gwen Stefani
The Sweetest Thing – Lauryn Hill
The Sweetest Thing – U2

Join the Wedding MusicLetter for the latest and trending wedding songs - every Wednesday.

FATHER-FIGURE DANCE

Songs Specifically Written for Dance
Dance With My Daughter – Jason Blaine
Father Daughter Dance – Craig Cardiff
This Dance – Scott Thomas Laughridge

Celebrating Love for Child
Butterfly Kisses – Bob Carlisle
Daddy's Girl – Channing Gillespie
I Loved Her First - Heartland
Moments into Memories – Will Dempsey
My Little Girl - Tim McGraw
The Man Who Loves You the Most – Zac Brown Band
Walk With You – Edwin McCain
You'll Always Be My Baby - Alan Jackson
Your Daddy Loves You – Gil Scott-Heron

Celebrating Love For Father-Figure
Daddy Dance With Me – Krystal Keith
Daddy's Little Girl – The Shires
Dads and Daughters – MaRynn Taylor
Good Hands – Johnny and Heidi
When God Made You My Father - Riley Roth

Putting Father-Figure in High Regard
First Man – Camila Cabello
Half the Man – Jennifer Smestad
Like My Daddy – LeNasia Tyson
Like My Father - Jax
Not All Heroes Wear Capes – Owl City
You'll Always Be My Hero – Ashley Marina

Celebrating Being There For Each Other
Call My Name – Lukas Graham
Good Hands - Kylie Morgan
I'll Be There – Jackson 5
One Call Away - Charlie Puth
She's Somebody's Daughter – Drew Baldridge
Stand By Me – Ben E. King
There You'll Be – Faith Hill
You'll Be In My Heart – Phil Collins
Your Joy – Chrisette Michele

Dance with Grandpa
Grandpa (Tell Me 'Bout The Good Old Days) - The Judds
Grandpa Told Me So - Kenny Chesney
Grandpas Baby Girl – Terry Wagenschutz

Celebrating Friendship
In My Life – Beatles
You're My Best Friend – Queen
You've Got A Friend – James Taylor

Unexpected & Fun Songs
Isn't She Lovely - Stevie Wonder
My Girl - Temptations
Shining Star – The Manhattans
Sweet Pea – Amos Lee
You Are The Sunshine Of My Life – Stevie Wonder
Your Mama Don't Dance – Loggins & Messina

Dedication To Child For The Future
Find Your Wings – Mark Harris
Forever Young – Rod Stewart
Humble And Kind – Tim McGraw
My Wish – Rascal Flatts

Celebrating Being Grown Up
Ready, Set, Don't Go – Billy Ray Cyrus feat. Miley Cyrus
There Goes My Life – Kenny Chesney
Time to Let Me Go – Quixotic Sound
You Can Let Go – Crystal Shawanda
You're A Big Girl Now – The Stylistics

Songs for Every Relationship
I'm Happy Just To Dance With You – Beatles
Lovely Day – Bill Withers
Over The Rainbow – Israel Kamakawiwo'ole
Teach Your Children – Crosby, Stills, Nash & Young
Three Little Birds – Bob Marley
What A Wonderful World – Louis Armstrong

Songs For A Single Dad
Babyfather – Sade
For My Daughter – Kane Brown
Rich Man - Little Big Town

Dance with Stepdad
My Boy (My Girl Version) – Elvie Shane
Step by Step – Brandon Davis

Dance with Father-In-Law
Family Affair - Mary J. Blige
Family Is Family - Kacey Musgraves
Hope You Dance - Lee Ann Womack

New Tracks You Need to Know
Anything Like You - Sam Derosa
Can She Have This Dance - Drew Baldridge
Counting My Blessings - Seph Schlueter
Father Daughter Song - White/Sayer
For The Both of Us - Dan + Shay
My Father's Daughter - Anne Wilson
Perfect Day - Al Green

Join the Wedding MusicLetter for the latest and trending wedding songs - every Wednesday.

MOTHER-FIGURE DANCE

Celebrating Love for Child
Boy – Caleb and Kelsey
Dance With Me, Baby – Toni Becker
Everything – Matthew John
He's Her Life – Waylon Nihipali
Mama's Hand – Queen Naija
No Matter What – Calum Scott
You're Gonna Be (Always Loved by Me) – Reba Mcentire

Celebrating Love for Mother-Figure
A Song For Mama – Boyz II Men
All To You – Scott Keo
I Love This Dance – Caleb Beachy
I Love You Mom – Jackson Nance
Mother – Michael Bublé

Celebrating Friendship
In My Life – Beatles
You're My Best Friend – Queen
You've Got A Friend – James Taylor

Putting Mother-Figure in High Regard
Hero – Mariah Carey
Mama Ain't Jesus – Jordan Rowe, Lainey Wilson
My Hero – Westlife
Perfect Fan – Backstreet Boys
superhuman – Bishop Briggs

Celebrating Being There For Each Other
Call My Name – Lukas Graham
I'll Be There – Jackson 5
One Call Away – Charlie Puth
Stand By Me – Ben E. King
There You'll Be – Faith Hill
You'll Be In My Heart – Phil Collins

Unexpected & Fun Songs
I'll Always Love My Mama – Intruders
Loves Me Like A Rock – Paul Simon
Mama – Lunchmoney Lewis
Sorry Mom – The Band CAMINO
Your Mama Don't Dance – Loggins & Messina

Dedication To Child For The Future
Days Like This – Van Morrison
Find Your Wings – Mark Harris
Forever Young – Rod Stewart
My Wish – Rascal Flatts
Simple Man – Shinedown

Songs for Every Relationship
I'm Happy Just To Dance With You – Beatles
Over The Rainbow – Israel Kamakawiwo'ole
Teach Your Children – Crosby, Stills, Nash & Young
What A Wonderful World – Louis Armstrong

Songs For A Single Mom
Mama Was Daddy Too – Tainted Lyric
Mother – Pink Floyd

Dance with Stepmom
Blended Family (What You Do For Love) – A. Keys, A$AP Rocky
My Boy – Elvie Shane
Step by Step – Brandon Davis

Dance with Mother-In-Law
Humble And Kind – Tim McGraw
I Hope You Dance – Lee Ann Womack
Most People Are Good – Luke Bryan
The Good Ones – Gabby Barrett

Dance with Grandma
Grandma's Garden – Zac Brown
Grandma's Hands – Bill Withers
Mamaw's House – Thomas Rhett, Morgan Wallen
You'll Be in My Heart – Brent Morgan

Dance with Sister
Brothers & Sisters – Coldplay
Come Dancing – Kinks
Rainbow Connection – JJ Heller

New Tracks You Need to Know
Boy Mama – Jason Blaine
Can She Have This Dance - Drew Baldridge
Growing Up Raising You – Gabby Barrett
Journey of You and I – Kodi Lee
Mama's Do – The Dryes
Mom Like You – Cade Thompson
Mother's Love – Soul Payn
Perfect Day – Al Green
Raised Up Right – Riley Green
Sun/Son – Jhené Aiko

Join the Wedding MusicLetter for the latest and trending wedding songs - every Wednesday.

MOTHER-DAUGHTER SONGS

Celebrating Love for Daughter
A Mother's Prayer - Celine Dion
Blue - Beyoncé
Child of Mine - Michaela Anne
Lady - Brett Young
Mother's Love - KEM
My Baby You - Marc Anthony
My Darling - Wilco
Sweetest Devotion - Adele
You Are the Sunshine of My Life - Stevie Wonder
You're Gonna Be - Reba McEntire

Celebrating Love for Mom
A Mother Like You - JJ Heller
Her - Anne-Marie
Like My Mother Does - Lauren Alaina
Mama - Il Divo
Mama - Spice Girls
Mama's Hand - Queen Naija
Mamas - Anne Wilson, Hillary Scott
Mother - Ashanti
My Mother's Hand - Jill Barber
The Best Day - Taylor Swift
When God Made You My Mother - Riley Roth

Honoring Your Mother
Always There - Canadian Tenors
Because You Loved Me - Celine Dion
Hero - Mariah Carey
In My Daughter's Eyes - Martina McBride
Mother - Sugarland
Mother Like Mine - Band Perry
My Hero - Westlife
Shiny - Sara Bareilles
Somebody's Hero - Jamie O'Neal
utopia - Lykke Li

Supporting Each Other
By Your Side - Sade
Call My Name – Lukas Graham
Count on Me - Bruno Mars
I Turn To You - Christina Aguilera
I Will Be Here - Steven Curtis Chapman
I'll Be - Reba McEntire
I'll Be There - Mariah Carey feat. Trey Lorenz
One Call Away – Charlie Puth
Promise - Tori Amos
Stand - Haley Smalls
There You'll Be – Faith Hill
Where You Lead, I Will Follow - Carole King

Celebrating Friendship
You're My Best Friend - Queen
You've Got A Friend - Carole King
You've Got A Friend – James Taylor
You've Got a Friend in Me - Randy Newman

Unexpected & Fun Songs
Baby Girl - Sugarland
Girl On Fire - Alicia Keys
Isn't She Lovely - Stevie Wonder
Mom - Meghan Trainor feat. Kelli Trainor
My Girl - Temptations
Teach Your Children - Crosby, Stills, Nash & Young
Thank You Mom - Good Charlotte

Wishing The Best for What's To Come
Cover Me In Sunshine - Pink, Willow Sage Hart
Little Things - One Direction
My Wish – Rascal Flatts
Promises - Jhene Aiko feat. NAMIKO & Miyagi
Slow Down - Nichole Nordeman
superhuman - Bishop

Growing Up
26 (Cents Sign) - Wilkinsons
Hey Ma I Made It - Ella Langley
Letting Go - Suzy Bogguss
Mama's Song - Carrie Underwood
My Song - H.E.R.
Never Grow Up - Taylor Swift
Slipping Through My Fingers - ABBA
Teenage Daughters - Martina McBride
You Don't Have To Let Go - Jessica Simpson
You Will Always Be (My Baby Girl) - Angel Sessions

Every Type of Relationship
I'm Happy Just To Dance With You – Beatles
Over The Rainbow – Israel Kamakawiwo'ole
What A Wonderful World – Louis Armstrong

Single Mom Appreciation
Mama Was Daddy Too – Tainted Lyric
Mother – Pink Floyd
You and Me Against the World – Helen Reddy

Dedication to Stepmom
Blended Family (What You Do For Love) – A. Keys, A$AP Rocky
My Boy (My Girl Version) – Elvie Shane
Step by Step – Brandon Davis

Dance with Mother-In-Law
I Hope You Dance – Lee Ann Womack
Love Can Build a Bridge – The Judds
The Good Ones – Gabby Barrett

New Tracks You Need to Know
Everything Was For Love - Carla Morrison
Girls - Rachel Platten
Good Mother - Stephanie Lambring
Light On In The Kitchen - Ashley McBryde
Live Forever - Kate Hudson
Mama's Do - The Dryes
Mama's Eyes - Tenille Arts
On Purpose (For My Future Daughter) - Bellah Mae
PROTECTOR - Beyonce, Rumi Carter
She's Superman - Taylor Austin Dye

22

Join the Wedding MusicLetter for the latest and trending wedding songs - every Wednesday.

FATHER-SON SONGS

Celebrating Love For Son
A Father's Love - Bucky Covington
Beautiful Boy (Darling Boy) - John Lennon
Father's Love - Bob Carlisle
He's Mine - Rodney Atkins
Here For You - Neil Young
Kooks - David Bowie
Little Guy - Gord Bamford
Little Man - Ian Munsick
Love Without End, Amen - George Strait
Packed Up My Love - Matt Hammitt
The Best Part Of Me - Lee Brice
The Man He Sees in Me - Luke Combs

Celebrating Love For Father
A Fathers Song - Allen Stone
Chasing Stars - Matteo Bocelli
Dad - Coleton Rubin
Dad - Tyler Wood
Father, Son - Peter Gabriel
Gettin' Older - Chris Young
Good Good Father - Chris Tomlin
Leader of the Band - Dan Fogelberg
Life Of A Salesman - Yellowcard
LIKE YOU - Aaron Cole, Tauren Wells, TobyMac
My Dad - Paul Petersen
My Old Man - Zac Brown Band
Not All Heroes Wear Capes - Owl City
Song for Dad - Keith Urban
That's My Job - Conway Twitty
Things Dads Do - Thomas Rhett
Things He Handed Down - Lady A

Father-Son Relationship
Cat's in the Cradle - Harry Chapin
Drinking Beer with Dad - Kid Rock
Drive (For Daddy Gene) - Alan Jackson
Father of Mine - Everclear
Father's Child - Michael Kiwanuka
Hey Dad - Tyler Booth
Independence Day - Bruce Springsteen
Landslide - Fleetwood Mac
Little Lion Man - Mumford & Sons
Man That Hung The Moon - Brantley Gilbert
My Father's House - Bruce Springsteen
My Old Man - Billy Raffoul
Raised Up Right - Riley Green
Reach the Pedals - Jesse Labelle
Sail To The Moon - Radiohead
The Best Day - George Strait
The Last Song - Elton John
What Makes a Man - Ben Rector, Thomas Rhett

Friendship
You're My Best Friend - Queen
You've Got A Friend - James Taylor
You've Got a Friend in Me – Randy Newman

Celebrating Being A Dad
Ain't Even Met You Yet - Chris Lane
Anything Like Me - Brad Paisley
It's A Boy - Slick Rick
Son - Mitch Rossell
Takes After You - ERNEST
The Day (That You Gave Me a Son) - Babyface
With Arms Wide Open - Creed
Without A Dad - Justin Champagne
You Will Always Be My Son - Caleb and Kelsey

Dad Getting Older
Dad's Sailboat - Walker Hayes
Father And Son - Boyzone
Father And Son - Cat Stevens
Hell Yeah - Neil Diamond
My Father's Eyes - Joshua Radin
Old Man - Beck
Old Man - Neil Young
Patches - Clarence Carter
Sometimes You Can't Make It On Your Own - U2
The Old Man - John McDermott
You Should Be Here - Cole Swindell

Advice To Son
Boy - Lee Brice
Carry on Wayward Son - Kansas
Father To Son - Queen
Letter 2 My Unborn - 2Pac
Letter to Me - Brad Paisley
Walk Like A Man - Bruce Springsteen

Dedication to Single Dad
Mr. Mom - Lonestar
Stay at Home Dad - Drew Baldridge

Dedication to Stepdad
He Didn't Have to Be - Brad Paisley
My Boy - Elvie Shane

Celebrating Grandfather
The Captain and The Kid - Jimmy Buffett
Tough - Brandon Davis

Wishing The Best for Child
Father To Son - Phil Collins
Forever Young - Rod Stewart
Like Father Like Son - The Game, Busta Rhymes
My Son - Eddie Montgomery
My Wish - Rascal Flatts

Loving Family
Family Man - Craig Campbell
Good Ol' Man - Drew Green
I Wish I Could Have Been There - John Anderson
Rich Man - Little Big Town

Supporting Each Other
Can You Feel The Love Tonight – Elton John
I Will Be Here - Steven Curtis Chapman
Just The Two Of Us - Will Smith
Wind Beneath My Wings - Gerald & Eddie LeVert

Join the Wedding MusicLetter for the latest and trending wedding songs - every Wednesday.

COMBINED PARENT DANCE SONGS

Loving A Child
Greatest Love Of All - Whitney Houston
Remember You Young - Thomas Rhett
Sunrise, Sunset - Cast from Fiddler on the Roof
Sweet Child O' Mine - Sheryl Crow
Tupelo Honey - Van Morrison
You Are The Sunshine Of My Life - Stevie Wonder
You'll Be In My Heart - Phil Collins

Loving Parents
God Only Knows - Kina Grannix, Imaginery Future
Hero - Mariah Carey
In Case You Don't Live Forever - Ben Platt
Not All Heroes Wear Capes - Owl City
Parent Song - Jeremy Zucker, Chelsea Cutler
The Best Day (Taylor's Version) - Taylor Swift
The House That Built Me - Miranda Lambert
Unsung Hero - for KING & COUNTRY

Wishing the Couple Well
Find Your Wings - Mark Harris
Forever Young - Andrea von Kampen
Forever Young - Rod Stewart
I Hope You Dance - Lee Ann Womack
Little Wonders - Rob Thomas
My Wish - Rascal Flatts

Enjoy Life
Humble and Kind - Tim McGraw
Kind & Generous - Nalie Merchant
Most People Are Good - Luke Bryan
Shower the People - James Taylor
Slow Down - Nichole Nordeman
Smile - Nat King Cole
The Greatest Day Of My Life - Zach Bryan
You're Gonna Miss This - Trace Adkins

Fun & Upbeat
93 Million Miles - Jason Mraz
Ain't That Love - Ray Charles
Count On Me - Bruno Mars
Dancing In The Moonlight - Toploader
Family Affair - Mary J. Blige
How Sweet It Is (To Be Loved By You) - Marvin Gaye
I Got You (I Feel Good) - James Brown
I'll Be Around - The Spinners
Let It Go - Demi Lovato
Lovely Day - Bill Withers
On Me - Thomas Rhett, Kane Brown, Ava Max
Parents Just Don't Understand - Jazzy Jeff & The Fresh Prince
Three Little Birds - Bob Marley

Feeling of Gratitude
Blessed - Elton John
In My Life - The Beatles
True Colors - Cyndi Lauper
Unforgettable - Nat King Cole, Natalie Cole

Every Type of Relationship
Constellations - Jack Johnson
If You Love Her - Forest Blakk
Next Thing You Know - Jordan Davis
Somewhere Over The Rainbow - Israel Kamakawiwo'ole
Teach Your Children - Crosby, Stills, Nash & Young
The Good Ones - Gabby Barrett
What A Wonderful World - Louis Armstrong
You Are My Sunshine - Zach Bryan

Always Being There
I'll Be There - Jackson 5
I'll Stand By You - The Pretenders
Never Alone - Jim Brickman, Lady A
One Call Away - Charlie Puth
Stand By Me - Ben E. King
There You'll Be - Faith Hill
You've Got A Freind - James Taylor

Join the Wedding MusicLetter for the latest and trending wedding songs - every Wednesday.

STEPDAD/STEPDAUGHTER SONGS

About Stepdads
He Didn't Have To Be – Brad Paisley
My Boy (My Girl Version)– Elvie Shane
Step by Step – Brandon Davis

Daughters Growing Up
Gracie – Ben Folds
It Won't Be Like This For Long – Darius Rucker
Story Of Love – Bon Jovi
Then They Do – Trace Adkins

A Loving Dad-Daughter Relationship
Beautiful Memory – Scott Keo
I Loved Her First – Heartland
Isn't She Lovely – Stevie Wonder
My Little Girl – Tim McGraw
Sweet Pea – Amos Lee

Songs About Superhero Dads
Hero – Mariah Carey
You'll Always Be My Hero – Ashley Marina

Wishing Your Stepdaughter The Best
Humble And Kind – Tim McGraw
I Hope You Dance – Lee Ann Womack
My Wish – Rascal Flatts

Songs About Being There
Call My Name – Lukas Graham
Count On Me – Bruno Mars
Never Alone – Jim Brickman Feat. Lady Antebellum
One Call Away – Charlie Puth
You're My Best Friend – Queen
You've Got A Friend – James Taylor

Songs About Letting Go
Time to Let Me Go – Quixotic Sound
You Can Let Go – Crystal Shawanda
You Don't Have to Let Go – Jessica Simpson

Gender-inclusive Songs
Forever Now – Michael Bublé

STEPMOM/STEPSON SONGS

About Stepparents
Blended Family (What You Do For Love) - Alicia Keys
He Didn't Have To Be – Brad Paisley
My Boy - Elvie Shane
Step by Step – Brandon Davis
Step Mom - Catie Turner

Wishing Stepson The Best
Humble And Kind – Tim McGraw
I Hope You Dance – Lee Ann Womack
My Wish – Rascal Flatts
You'll Be in My Heart – Brent Morgan

Being There
Call My Name – Lukas Graham
Count On Me – Bruno Mars
I'll Be There – Jackson 5
I'll Stand By You – The Pretenders
Lean On Me – Bill Withers
One Call Away – Charlie Puth

Sons Growing Up
Boy – Caleb + Kelsey
Slow Down – Nichole Nordeman
Tough Little Boys – Gary Allan

A Loving Stepmother-Son Relationship
I Love This Dance – Caleb Beachy
I Love You Mom – Jackson Nance
Mama's Boy – Ryan Griffin
The Perfect Fan – Backstreet Boys

Gender-inclusive Songs
Everything – Matthew John
Forever Now – Michael Bublé
No Matter What – Calum Scott

Join the Wedding MusicLetter for the latest and trending wedding songs - every Wednesday.

IN-LAW DANCE SONGS

Family Theme
Blended Family - Alicia Keys, A$AP Rocky
Chosen Family - Rina Sawayama
Family - Dolly Parton
Family - Drew Holcomb & The Neighbors
Family Affair - Mary J Blige
Family Is Family - Kacey Musgraves
Family Man - Fleetwood Mac
Family Portrait - P!nk
Family Tradition - Hank Williams, Jr.
Keep The Family Close - Drake
Kooks - David Bowie
Love Can Build A Bridge - The Judds
Rich Man - Little Big Town
We Are Family - Sister Sledge

Fun & Unexpected
A Wink And A Smile - Harry Connick Jr.
Ain't That Love - Ray Charles
Don't Stop Believin' - Journey
Don't Worry, Be Happy - Bobby McFerrin
Every Little Thing She Does Is Magic - The Police
Happy - Pharrell Williams
Home - Edward Sharpe and the Magnetic Zeros
Home - Phillip Phillips
How Sweet It Is (To Be Loved By You) - James Taylor
I Can See Clearly Now - Johnny Nash
Lean On Me - Club Nouveau
Let's Dance - David Bowie
Seasons Of Love - Cast Of Rent
Smile - Nat King Cole
Smile - Uncle Kracker
Somebody To Love - Queen
The Way You Look Tonight - Frank Sinatra

Every Type of Relationship
I Just Want To Dance With You - George Strait
Only Time - Enya
Over the Rainbow - Israel Kamakawiwo'ole
Teach Your Children - Crosby, Stills, Nash & Young
These Are the Days - Van Morrison
Three Little Birds - Bob Marley
What A Wonderful - Louis Armstrong
Wildfire - Michael Martin Murphey
Wonderful Tonight - Eric Clapton

Parent-Child Relationship
Blessed - Elton John
Isn't She Lovely - Stevie Wonder
Landslide - Fleetwood Mac
Like Jesus Does - Eric Church
Sweet Child O' Mine - Guns N' Roses
Take Good Care Of My Baby - Bobby Vee
Tell Me Twice - Chayce Beckham
The Good Ones - Gabby Barrett
Treat Her Right - Sawyer Brown
You Are My Sunshine - Morgane & Chris Stapleton

Being There For Each Other
Call My Name - Lukas Graham
Count On Me - Whitney Houston, CeCe Winans
Hold My Hand - Hootie & The Blowfish
I'll Be There - Jackson 5
I'll Be There - Mariah Carey
I'll Stand by You - Josh Groban, Helene Fischer
I'll Stand By You - The Pretenders
I'm Happy Just To Dance With You - The Beatles
Lean on Me - Bill Withers
On Me - Thomas Rhett, Kane Brown, Ava Max
Stand By Me - Ben E. King
There You'll Be - Faith Hill
You've Got A Friend - James Taylor
You've Got a Friend in Me - Randy Newman

Loving Each Other
Because You Loved Me - Celine Dion
Can You Feel The Love Tonight - Elton John
Have I Told You Lately - Rod Stewart
Heroes - Haley Reinhart
In My Life - The Beatles
Life Is Wonderful - Jason Mraz
Ordinary Miracle - Sarah McLachlan
Remedy - Adele
Time After Time - Cyndi Lauper
You'll Be In My Heart - Phil Collins

Good Will for the Future
Days Like This - Van Morrison
Forever Young - Andrea von Kampen
Forever Young - Rod Stewart
Humble and Kind - Tim McGraw
I Hope You Dance - Lee Ann Womack
I Wish You Love - Natalie Cole
Let Your Love Flow - Bellamy Brothers
Little Wonders - Rob Thomas
My Wish – Rascal Flatts
The Best Is Yet To Come - Michael Buble
Wildflowers - Tom Petty

Join the Wedding MusicLetter for the latest and trending wedding songs - every Wednesday.

BRIDESMAIDS SONGS

Bridesmaids Processional
10,000 Hours (Piano) - Dan + Shay & Justin Bieber
A Thousand Years (Remix) - The Piano Guys
A Whole New World (End Title) - ZAYN & Zhavia Ward
Best Friend for Life - Grace Leer
Bloom - The Paper Kites
Canon in D - Brooklyn Duo
Falling Like the Stars (Acoustic) - Amber Leigh Irish
Grow Old With You - Ortopilot
Here Comes the Sun - Boyce Avenue
Higher Love - James Vincent McMorrow
I Get to Love You - Ruelle
I'm Gonna Be (500 Miles) - Sleeping At Last
Only Girl (In the World) - Boyce Avenue
She Is Love - Parachute
Stand - Me - Skylar Grey
There She Goes - Sixpence None The Richer
Truly Madly Deeply (Acoustic) - Plamina
Turning Page (Instrumental) - Sleeping At Last
What a Wonderful World - Sawyer Fredericks
Wildest Dreams - Duomo
You Are My Sunshine - Music Travel Love
You Are The Best Thing - Bridesmaid Quartet
Yours (Wedding Edition) - Russell Dickerson

Bridesmaids Introductions
Bang Bang - Jessie J & Ariana Grande & Nicki Minaj
Barbie Girl - by Aqua
Been Like This - Meghan Trainor, T-Pain
Bridesmaids - Kylie Morgan
Bridesmaids - Tyra Madison
Buttons - The Pussycat Dolls
Dangerous - Kardinal Offishall, Akon
Family Affair - Mary J. Blige
Fight Song - Rachel Platten
Girls Like You - Maroon 5 feat. Cardi B
Independent Women, Pt. 1 - Destiny's Child
Let Me Blow Ya Mind - Eve and Gwen Stefani
Lovely Day - Bill Withers
One, Two Step - Ciara feat. Missy Elliott
Only Girl (In The World) - Rihanna
That's My Girl - Fifth Harmony
Thunder - Imagine Dragons
Wrecking Ball - Miley Cyrus

Bridesmaids Party Songs
7 rings - Ariana Grande
A Thousand Miles - Vanessa Carlton
Bad Guy - Billie Eilish
Bad Blood - Taylor Swift
Bang Bang - Jessie J, Ariana Grande, Nicki Minaj
Best Friend - Saweetie feat. Doja Cat
Bodak Yellow - Cardi B
Born This Way - Lady Gaga
Can't Hold Us Down - Christina Aguilera featuring Lil' Kim
Confident - Demi Lovato
Dancing Queen - ABBA
Diamonds - Rihanna
Edge of Seventeen - Stevie Nicks
Espresso - Sabrina Carpenter
Flowers - Miley Cyrus
Girl on Fire - Alicia Keys
Girls Just Want To Have Fun - Cyndi Lauper
Glamorous - Fergie feat. Ludacris
Good as Hell - Lizzo
good 4 u - Olvia Rodrigo
greedy - Tate McRae
Hold On - Wilson Phillips
I Like That - Cardi B, Bad Bunny, J Balvin
I Love It - Icona Pop, Charli XCX
II MOST WANTED - Beyoncé, Miley Cyrus
Just a Girl - No Doubt
Man! I Feel Like A Woman - Shania Twain
No Scrubs - TLC
Not Tonight (Remix) - Lil' Kim
Pretty Girl Rock - Keri Hilson
Promiscuous - Nelly Furtado feat. Timbaland
Respect - Aretha Franklin
Roar - Katy Perry
Run the World (Girls) - Beyoncé
Shake It Off - Taylor Swift
Single Ladies (Put A Ring On It) - Beyoncé
Stronger - Britney Spears
Stronger - Kelly Clarkson
That's My Girl - Fifth Harmony
Unwritten - Natasha Bedingfield
Up - Cardi B
Video - Indie.Arie
Wannabe - Spice Girls
What's Up? - 4 Non Blondes
Where My Girls At - 702
Without Me - Halsey
Woman - Doja Cat
You Oughta Know - Alanis Morissette

Join the Wedding MusicLetter for the latest and trending wedding songs - every Wednesday.

GROOMSMEN SONGS

Groomsmen Processional
A Drop In The Ocean – Ron Pope
A Million Dreams – The Piano Guys
Falling Like the Stars (Acoustic) – Amber Leigh Irish
Here Comes the Sun – Boyce Avenue
How Long Will I Love You (acoustic) – Matt Johnson
I Don't Want To Miss A Thing – Music Travel Love
Jurassic Park Theme – Vitamin String Quartet
Kiss The Girl – Brent Morgan
Latch (Acoustic) – Sam Smith
Like I'm Gonna Lose You – Jasmine Thompson
Love Me Like You Do – Brooklyn Duo
Love Story – Tyler Ward, Karis, Ray Lorraine
Once In A Lifetime – Landon Austin
One of Mine – Drew Green
Quit You – Kameron Marlowe
Rest of Your Life – David J
Simply The Best – Billianne
Stand By Me – Skylar Grey
Turning Page (Instrumental) – Sleeping At Last
Until I Found You (Piano Version) – Stephen Sanchez
Waiting On You – Jon B, Tank
Wildest Dreams – Dallas String Quartet
Worth the Wait – Spencer Crandall
You Are My Sunshine – Kina Grannis
You Are The Best Thing – Bridesmaid Quartet
You're The One I Want – Caroline Kole, Dylan Rockoff
Yours (Wedding Edition) – Russell Dickerson

Groomsmen Introductions
All I Do Is Win – DJ Khaled
Back In Black – AC/DC
Bring Em Out – T.I.
Enter Sandman – Metallica
Here Comes The Hotstepper – Ini Kamoze
Hypnotize – The Notorious B.I.G.
Let's Get Married – Bleachers
Lose Yourself – Eminem
Mo Bamba – Sheck Wes
My House – Flo Rida
NFL Theme Song – Instrumental All Stars
On Top Of The World – Imagine Dragons
Sabotage – Beastie Boys
Sharp Dressed Man – ZZ Top
Star Wars (Main Theme) – John Williams
Suit & Tie – Justin Timberlake, Jay-Z
The Man – Aloe Blacc
Theme from The Dukes of Hazzard (Good Ol' Boys) – Walon Jennings
Thunderstruck – AC/DC
Turn Down For What – DJ Snake, Lil Jon
Walk It Out – Unk

Groomsmen Party Songs
1985 – Bowling For Soup
99 Problems – Jay-Z
A Bar Song (Tipsy) – Shaboozey
All The Small Things – blink-182
Betty (Get Money) – Yung Gravy
California Love – 2Pac, Roger, Dr. Dre
Can't Hold Us – Macklemore & Ryan Lewis
Church Clap – KB
Heartless – Kanye West
Here I Am – Rick Ross feat. Nelly & Avery Storm
Hip Hop Hooray – Naughty – Nature
Hotel Room Service – Pitbull
I Want It That Way – Backstreet Boys
Int'l Players Anthem (I Choose You) – UGK (Underground Kingz)
Jump Around – House of Pain
Lean Back – Fat Joe, Remy Ma, and Terror Squad
Like That – Future, Metro Boomin & Kendrick Lamar
Live Your Life – T.I., Rihanna
Lovin On Me – Jack Harlow
Low – Flo Rida, T-Pain
MILLION DOLLAR BABY – Tommy Richman
Mr. Brightside – The Killers
My Own Worst Enemy – Lit
No Hands – Waka Flocka Flame, Roscoe Dash
Not Like Us – Kendrick Lamar
Ocean Avenue – Yellowcard
Party Up (Up in Here) – DMX
Pepas – Farruko
Pursuit of Happiness (Nightmare) – Kid Cudi, Ratatat, MGMT
Shake Dat Ass (Twerk Song) – Bossman Dlow
Shots – LMFAO ft. Lil Jon
Sugar, We're Goin Down – Fall Out Boy
The Spins – Mac Miller
Tipsy – J-Kwon
Trap Queen – Fetty Wap
Year 3000 – Jonas Brothers

Join the Wedding MusicLetter for the latest and trending wedding songs - every Wednesday.

SISTER SONGS

About Sisters
Baby Sister – Dolly Parton
Call Your Sister – Taylor Edwards
Call Your Sister (Sister Version) - Taylor Edwards
Dance Little Sister – The Rolling Stones
Dear Sister – The Pretty Reckless
Hey, Soul Sister – Train
My Sister - Reba McEntire
My Sister - Shaybo and Jorja Smith
My Sister Rose - 10,000 Maniacs
Oh, Sister – Bob Dylan
Older Sister – Carly Simon
On The Ride – Aly & AJ
Sister – Angel Olsen
Sister – Dave Matthews & Tim Reynolds
Sister – K.Flay
Sister – Mickey Guyton
Sister (I'd Choose You For My Friend) – Valerie DeLaCruz
Sister Blister – Alanis Morissette
Sister Golden Hair – America
Sister Oh Sister – Rosanne Cash
Sister's Love - Rebecca Winckworth
Sisters – Sweethearts Of The Rodeo
Sisters – The Puppini Sisters
Sisters Are Doin' It For Themselves – Franklin, Eurythmics
Sisters Of The Moon – Fleetwood Mac
True Sisters – Cast – Sofia the First
Two Sisters – The Kinks
You Are My Sister – Antony And The Johnsons

Being Friends
Best Friend - Aaliyah feat Missy Elliott
Best Friend - Saweetie feat. Doja Cat (Hip Hop
Best Friend – Brandy
Best Friend – Missy Elliott feat Aaliyah
II MOST WANTED - Beyoncé, Miley Cyrus
My Same – Adele
True Friend – Hannah Montana
What About Your Friends – TLC
You've Got A Friend – Carole King
You've Got A Friend In Me – Randy Newman

About Girls
Bad Girls – Donna Summer
Girls - Rachel Platten
Girls Just Want to Have Fun – Cyndi Lauper
Girls Need Girls - Sophia Scott
Most Girls – Hailee Steinfeld
Sorority Girl – Luke Bryan
This One's For The Girls - Martina McBride

Protector
Angel – Natasha Bedingfield
Sanctuary – Nashville Cast

Being There For Each Other
Count On Me – Bruno Mars
Count On Me – Whitney Houston & CeCe Winans
I Got You - Leona Lewis
I'll Be Here - Colbie Caillat, Sheryl Crow
I'll Be There For You – The Rembrandts
I'll Stand By You – The Pretenders
I'll Take Care of You – The Chicks
Lean On Me – Bill Withers
There You'll Be – Faith Hill
When You Need It - Tenille Townes, Wrabel
Wind Beneath My Wings – Bette Midler
You Got Me – Gavin DeGraw

Celebrating Family
Family Affair – Mary J. Blige
Good Friend And A Glass Of Wine – LeAnn Rimes
Just Fine – Mary J. Blige

Well Wishes
Best Days – Graham Colton
Comfort – Deb Talan
Exhale (Shoop Shoop) – Whitney Houston
For Good – Kristin Chenoweth & Idina Menzel
I Wish – Heather Headley
Kind and Generous – Natalie Merchant
Look For The Good – Jason Mraz
My Wish – Rascal Flatts
Time Of Our Lives – Tyrone Wells
Wildflowers – Tom Petty

Ruling The World
Can't Hold Us Down – Christina Aguilera
Diamonds - Rihanna
Formation – Beyoncé
Girl On Fire - Alicia Keys
Highwomen – The Highwomen
Spice Up Your Life – Spice Girls
Superwoman – Alicia Keys
Video – India.Arie
We Got the World - Icona Pop

Growing Up Together
Beautiful Thing – Grace VanderWaal
Come Some Rainy Day – Wynonna
Hey, I'm Just Like You - Tegan and Sara
I Don't Care – Shakespears Sister
Oldest Daughter - Makayla Lynn
Seamless – Sabrina Carpenter
Shadow – Ashlee Simpson
Whenever You Remember Carrie Underwood
You And Me – Rosie Thomas

Join the Wedding MusicLetter for the latest and trending wedding songs - every Wednesday.

SISTER & BROTHER SONGS

Dedication to Brother
Brotherly Love – Keith Whitley, Earl Thomas Conley
He Ain't Heavy, He's My Brother – The Hollies
Hey Brother - Avicii
Hey Brother - Dan Tyminski
Little Brothers – Phineas and Ferb
My Brother Taught Me How to Swim – Passion Pit

Dedication to Sister
All My Life – Flo Rida
Come Some Rainy Day – Wynonna
Dance Little Sister - Rolling Stones
Dance Little Sister – Terence Trent D'Arby
Isn't She Lovely – Stevie Wonder
Look at Little Sister – Stevie Ray Vaughan
My Big Sister – Barenaked Ladies
My Sister – Juliana Hatfield Three
My Sister – Reba McEntire
Oh, Sister – Bob Dylan
Older Sister – Carly Simon
Sister - Dave Matthews & Tim Reynolds
Sister – Nixons
Sister Christian – Night Ranger
Sister Oh Sister – Rodney Crowell, Mary Karr, R. Cash

About Girls
American Girl – Tom Petty
Dancing Queen – ABBA
Girl on Fire – Alicia Keys

Growing Up
American Honey – Lady A
It Don't Have to Change – John Legend
We Are Going to Be Friends – White Stripes
We Were Just Kids – Clean Bandit
Whenever You Remember – Carrie Underwood
Who Says You Can't Go Home – Bon Jovi, J. Nettles

Friendship
Best Friend – Brandy
Best Friends – Missy Elliott feat. Aaliyah
Brother – Kodaline
My Best Friend – Weezer
You're My Best Friend – Queen
You've Got A Friend – James Taylor
You've Got A Friend in Me – Randy Newman

Hope for the Future
Better Place – Rachel Platten
Brother Sister – Brand New Heavies
Brothers & Sisters - Coldplay
Don't Forget to Remember Me – Carrie Underwood
Have It All – Jason Mraz
I Hope You Dance – Lee Ann Womack
I Wish You Love – Nat King Cole
Into the Mystic – Van Morrison
Just Fine – Mary J. Blige
Landslide – Fleetwood Mac
My Wish – Rascal Flatts
Over the Rainbow – Israel Kamakawiwo'ole
Wildflowers – Tom Petty

Brother Sister Relationship
Boss of Me – They Might Be Giants
Brother Mine – Suzanne Vega
Brother, Sister – Beta Radio
Come Dancing - Kinks
Footprints – Molly Kate Kestner
I Learned From You – Miley Cyrus and Billy Ray Cyrus
Orange Sky - Alexi Murdoch
Pollyanna's Shadow - Howie D
We Are Family – Sister Sledge

Fun & Unexpected
CAN'T STOP THE FEELING! – Justin Timberlake
Come On Get Happy – Partridge Family
Happier – Marshmello, Bastille
Happy – Pharrell Williams
Mr. Blue Sky - Weezer
Mr. Blue Sky – Electric Light Orchestra
Rainbow Connection - Brian McKnight
Rainbow Connection - JJ Heller
Rainbow Connection – Kermit the Frog
White Wedding – Billy Idol

Supporting Each Other
Count On Me – Bruno Mars
Count On Me – Whitney Houston & CeCe Winans
Have I Told You Lately – Rod Stewart
Hero – Mariah Carey
I'll Be Here - Colbie Caillat, Sheryl Crow
I'll Be There – Jackson 5
I'll Be There for You – The Rembrandts
Keep Holding On – Avril Lavigne
Lean On Me – Bill Withers
Love You True (String Sessions) - Lydia Luce
Stand By Me – Ben E King
There You'll Be – Faith Hill
When You Need It - Tenille Townes feat. Wrabel
You'll Be In My Heart – Phil Collins
Your Guardian Angel - Red Jumpsuit Apparatus

Join the Wedding MusicLetter for the latest and trending wedding songs - every Wednesday.

BROTHER SONGS

Loving Your Brother
Brother – Alice In Chains
Brother's Keeper - DaBaby
It's Not Living (If It's Not With You) - The 1975
Me And Baby Brother – War
My Brother - Sam Tompkins
My Brother – Justin Hayward & John Lodge

Being There
Brother - Home Free
Brother - Isaiah Paul
Brother - NEEDTOBREATHE
He Ain't Heavy He's My Brother – Neil Diamond
He Ain't Heavy, He's My Brother - The Hollies

Be Your Own Man
Brother - Brendan Kelly
I Lived - OneRepublic
Little Brother - Hootie & the Blowfish
My Little Brother - Art Brut
Superheroes - The Script

Brotherhood
Blood Brothers - Luke Bryan
Blood Brothers - Papa Roach
Blood Brothers – Bruce Springsteen
Brothers - LOCASH
Brothers in Arms – DAGames
Brothers in Arms – Dire Straits
Hey Big Brother – Rare Earth
Hey Brother – Avicii
range brothers - Baby Keem & Kendrick Lamar

Special Bond
Big Brother – Kanye West
Boys Are Back In Town – Thin Lizzy
Brother - Kodaline
Brother – Brett Eldredge
Song for My Brother – Carlos Santana

Growing Up
American Kids - Kenny Chesney
Brother Mine – Suzanne Vega
The Greatest Discovery – Elton John
The Suburbs – Arcade Fire

Fun & Unexpected
ABC - Jackson Five
Congratulations - Post Malone feat. Quavo
Crazy Rap (Colt 45 & 2 Zig Zags) - Afroman
Eye of the Tiger - Survivor
MMMBop – Hanson
My Brother's a Basehead – De La Soul
Regulate - Warren G, Nate Dogg
Seven Nation Army - The White Stripes
Teenage Dirtbag - Wheatus

WEDDING PARTY DANCE SONGS

Line/Group Dances
Achy Breaky Heart - Billy Ray Cyrus
Boot Scootin' Boogie - Brooks & Dunn
Cha Cha Slide - DJ Casper
Cupid Shuffle - Cupid
No rompas mi corazón - Caballo Dorado
Teach Me How to Dougie - Cali Swag District
The Git Up - Blanco Brown
Tootsee Roll - 69 Boyz
Twist and Shout - The Beatles
Wagon Wheel - Darius Rucker
Wobble - V.I.C.

Classic Party Hits
Dance With Me Tonight - Olly Murs
Dancing Queen - ABBA
Danza Kuduro - Don Omar, Lucenzo
Get Down Tonight - KC and The Sunshine Band
Hooked On A Feeling - Blue Swede
I Wanna Dance With Somebody - Whitney Houston
Let's Get Married (ReMarqable Remix) - Jagged Edge
Let's Groove - Earth, Wind & Fire
Mr. Blue Sky - Electric Light Orchestra
My Boo - Ghost Town DJs
Now That We Found Love - Heavy D. & The Boyz
September - Earth, Wind & Fire
Stayin' Alive - The Bee Gees
Thunderstruck - AC/DC
Tongue Tied - Grouplove
Wanna Be Startin' Somethin' - Michael Jackson
You Should Be Dancing - Bee Gees

Romance
At Last - Etta James
Here On Out - Dave Matthews Band
I Love You Always Forever - Betty Who
May I Have This Dance - Francis and the Lights
Nobody But You - Blake Shelton & Gwen Stefani
Perfect - Ed Sheeran, Beyoncé
Speechless - Dan + Shay
Stand By Me - Ben E. King
Tennessee Whiskey - Chris Stapleton
Thank God - Kane Brown & Katelyn Brown
Thinking Out Loud - Ed Sheeran
When You Say Nothing At All - Alison Krauss
You Are The Reason - Calum Scott & Leona Lewis

Celebrating Family & Friends
All My Rowdy Friends Are Coming Over - H. Williams Jr.
Beer With My Friends - Kenny Chesney, Old Dominion
Family - Drew Holcomb & The Neighbors
Friends In Low Places - Garth Brooks
Good Things - BoDeans
In My Life - Beatles
Kinfolks - Sam Hunt
Me And My Gang - Rascal Flatts
these are my friends - lovelytheband
These Are My People - Rodney Atkins
We Are Family - Sister Sledge
With A Little Help From My Friends - Joe Cocker

Modern Party Hits
Bailondo Bachata - Chayanne
Can't Dance - Cooper Alan
Can't Stop The Feeling! - Justin Timberlake
Club Can't Handle Me - Flo Rida, David Guetta
Dance The Night - Dua Lipa
Dynamite - Taio Cruz
Everybody (Backstreet's Back) - Backstreet Boys
Feel So Close - Calvin Harris
Forever - Chris Brown
I Gotta Feeling - Black Eyed Peas
I'm Good (Blue) - David Guetta, Bebe Rexha
Just Dance - Lady Gaga
Kings & Queens - Ava Max
Let's Get Married - Bleachers
Mi Gente - J Balvin, Willy William
On Top Of The World - Imagine Dragons
One More Time - Daft Punk
Party Rock Anthem - LMFAO
Pink Party Club - Chapell Roan
Raise Your Glass - P!NK
Say Hey (I Love You) - Michael Franti & Spearhead
Sexy And I Know It - LMFAO
Shut Up And Dance - Walk The Moon
Taki Taki - DJ Snake, Selena Gomez, Ozuna and Cardi B
Texas Hold 'Em - Beyonce
This Is How We Do It - Montell Jordan
Timber - Pitbull, Ke$Ha
Turn Down for What - DJ Snake, Lil Jon
We Found Love - Rihanna, Calvin Harris
Yeah - Usher
Yeah 3x - Chris Brown

Join the Wedding MusicLetter for the latest and trending wedding songs - every Wednesday.

ANNIVERSARY DANCE SONGS

Anniversary Theme
Anniversary - Duran Duran
Anniversary - Tony Toni Tone
Anniversary Song – Cowboy Junkies
Anniversary Song – Eva Cassidy
Anniversary Waltz - Eddy Howard
Happy Anniversary - Kelly Morrison
Happy Anniversary – Ray, Goodman & Brown

Celebrating Your Partner
Because You Loved Me – Celine Dion
Best Friends - Eric Paslay
Biggest Part Of Me – Ambrosia
I Could Not Ask For More – Edwin McCain
I Was Made for Loving You – Tori Kelly, Ed Sheeran
I'm Yours – Jason Mraz
Just The Two Of Us - G. Washington Jr., Bill Withers
My Kind Of Woman / My Kind Of Man – Loveless & Gill
Perfect – Ed Sheeran with Beyonce
Still In Love – Lionel Richie
Wonderful Tonight – Eric Clapton
World For Two – King Calaway
You Are The Reason – Calum Scott, Leona Lewis
You Just Get Better All The Time – Tim McGraw
Your Song – Elton John

Celebrating a Life of Love
100 Years - Five For Fighting
After All These Years – Journey
As Time Goes By – Anna Nalick
Can't Remember Never Loving You – Ian Janes
Country Gold – Anne Wilson, Jordan Davis
Here, There and Everywhere - The Beatles
I'd Love You All Over Again – Alan Jackson
In My Life – The Beatles
Kept Every Vow - Spencer Crandall
Love You Like I Used To - Russell Dickerson
Love You Still (abcdefu romantic version) - Tyler Shaw
Our Song – Tank
Our Song – Willie Nelson
Remember The Time - The Teskey Brothers
Still The One - Orleans
Through The Years – Rascal Flatts
Times Of Your Life – Paul Anka
What I Got - SmithField
You Decorated My Life - Kenny Rogers
You're Still The One - Shania Twain
You're Still The One – Teddy Swims

The Beginning of Forever
99 Years – Josh Groban, Jennifer Nettles
A Moment Like This – Kelly Clarkson
Could I Have This Dance – Anne Murray
Endless Love – Lionel Richie & Diana Ross
Forever And Ever, Amen – Randy Travis
Forever And For Always – Shania Twain
Forever My Lady – Jodeci
From The Ground Up – Dan + Shay
Grow Old With Me – Mary Chapin Carpenter
Let's Stay Together – Al Green
Never Not Loving You - Johnny and Heidi
On This Day – David Pomeranz
Porch Swing - Taylor Hicks
Saving Forever For You – Shanice
The Rest of Our Life – Tim McGraw & Faith Hill
Truly Madly Deeply – Savage Garden
We've Only Just Begun – Carpenters
When I Said I Do – Clint Black and Lisa Hartman Black

Fun & Unexpected
(I've Had) The Time Of My Life – Bill Medley, Jennifer Warnes
A Thing Called Love – Johnny Cash
Forever Young – Rod Stewart
Honeymoon Feelin' – Roy Clark
I Got You Babe – Sonny & Cher
It Had To Be You – Harry Connick Jr.
Just The Way You Are – Bruno Mars
Just to Say I Love You – Michael Franti & Spearhead
L-O-V-E – Nat King Cole
Love Will Keep Us Together – Captain & Tennille
My Way – Frank Sinatra
This Will Be (An Everlasting Love) - Natalie Cole
When I'm Sixty-Four - The Beatles
You Make Loving Fun – Fleetwood Mac
You're The First, The Last, My Everything – Barry White

Love & Commitment
All My Life – America
Always – Bon Jovi
Always Remember Us This Way – Lady Gaga
As Long As You Love Me – Backstreet Boys
Die A Happy Man – Thomas Rhett
Have I Told You Lately – Van Morrison
How Deep Is Your Love – Bee Gees
I Love You – Climax Blues Band
Just The Way You Are – Billy Joel
Love Like Crazy – Lee Brice
More Than Words – Extreme
Stay With You – John Legend
That's How Love Is Made - The War and Treaty
Tonight, I Celebrate My Love – P.Bryson, R. Flack
Unchained Melody – The Righteous Brothers
You & I – Avant feat. KeKe Wyatt

BOUQUET TOSS SONGS

All About The Girls
Ayy Ladies - Travis Porter feat. Tyga
Bad Girls - Donna Summer
California Gurls - Katy Perry
Da Girls - Ciara
Fly Girl - FLO, Missy Elliott
Girl On Fire - Alicia Keys
Girls - Rita Ora feat. Cardi B, Bebe Rexha & Charli XCX
Girls Got Rhythm - AC/DC
Girls, Girls, Girls - Motley Crue
Grrrls - Lizzo
Hollaback Girl - Gwen Stefani
I'm a Lady - Meghan Trainor
Just A Girl - No Doubt
Luck Be A Lady - Frank Sinatra
Lucky Girl - Carlina
Only Girl In The World - Rihanna
Single White Female - Chely Wright
THE GIRLS (BLACKPINK THE GAME OST) - BLACKPINK
This One's For The Girls - Martina McBride
Uptown Girl - Billy Joel
Where My Girls At - 702
Where the Country Girls At - T. Adkins, L. Bryan & Pitbull
Where Them Girls At - David Guetta

It's About To Go Down
Another One Bites The Dust - Queen
Eye Of The Tiger - Survivor
Girlfight - Brooke Valentine
Hit Me With Your Best Shot - Pat Benatar
Love Is A Battlefield - Pat Benatar
Move B***h - Ludacris
One Way Or Another - Blondie
Throwin' Elbows - Excision & Space Laces

Flaunt What God Gave You
Applause - Lady Gaga
Been Like This - Meghan Trainor, T-Pain
Dangerous - Kardinal Offishall, Akon
Don't Cha - Pussycat Dolls ft. Busta Rhymes
Fancy - Iggy Azalea feat. Charli XCX
Glamorous - Fergie feat. Ludacris
Good as Hell - Lizzo
Milkshake - Kelis
My Lovin' (You're Never Gonna Get It) - En Vogue
Oh, Pretty Woman - Roy Orbison
Pressure - Ari Lennox
Pretty Girl Rock - Keri Hilson
Pretty Girls - Britney Spears & Iggy Azalea
Sexy Chick - David Guetta with Akon
Worth It - Fifth Harmony feat. Kid Ink
Yo Perreo Sola - Bad Bunny
You Sexy Thing - Hot Chocolate

Women Rule The World
Badass Woman - Meghan Trainor
Bang Bang - Jessie J, Ariana Grande and Nicki Minaj
Can't Hold Us Down - Christina Aguilera
Formation - Beyonce
Girl Gang - Gin Wigmore
Independent Women - Destiny's Child
Lady Marmalade - Christina Aguilera & Friends
Man! I Feel Like A Woman - Shania Twain
Not Tonight (Remix) - Lil' Kim
Powerful Women - Pitbull, Dolly Parton
Respect - Aretha Franklin
Run The World (Girls) - Beyoncé
WOMAN'S WORLD - Katy Perry

Having a Good Time
Crazy Angels - Carrie Underwood
Date With The Night - Yeah Yeah Yeahs
Girls Just Want to Have Fun - Cyndi Lauper
Girls Night Out - Charli XCX
I'm Coming Out - Diana Ross
It's Raining Men - The Weather Girls
Jumpin' Jumpin' - Destiny's Child
Ladies Night - Kool & The Gang
Let's Get Loud - Jennifer Lopez
Pink Friday Girls - Nicki Minaj
Wannabe - Spice Girls

Your BFFs
Bridesmaids - Kylie Morgan
Bridesmaids - Tyra Madison
7 Rings - Ariana Grande
Best Friend - Shania Twain
That's My Girl - Fifth Harmony

It's My Turn
2 Be Loved (Am I Ready) - Lizzo
About Damn Time - Lizzo
Any Man of Mine - Shania Twain
Call Me Maybe - Carly Rae Jepsen
CUFF IT - Beyonce
Dancing Queen - ABBA
Dear Future Husband - Meghan Trainor
Dog Days Are Over - Florence + The Machine
Ex's & Oh's - Elle King
Flowers - Miley Cyrus
Gimme! Gimme! Gimme! (A Man After Midnight) - ABBA
I Wanna Dance with Somebody - Whitney Houston
I Will Survive - Gloria Gaynor
Love On Top - Beyonce
Marry You - Bruno Mars
Mr Right - Mae Stephens and Meghan Trainor
One Less Lonely Girl - Justin Bieber
Paper Rings - Taylor Swift
Single Ladies (Put A Ring On It) - Beyoncé

Join the Wedding MusicLetter for the latest and trending wedding songs - every Wednesday.

GARTER REMOVAL SONGS

All About the Bride
Bad Girls - Donna Summer
Beautiful - Snoop Dogg
Brick House - The Commodores
Dance for You - Beyonce
Dangerous Woman - Ariana Grande
Foxey Lady - Jimi Hendrix
Hot Legs - Rod Stewart
Lady Marmalade - Christina Aguilera & Friends
Legs - ZZ Top
Woman - Doja Cat

All About the Groom
Bad Boys – Inner Circle
Best I Ever Had – Drake
Better Man – Leon Bridges
Big Pimpin' – Jay-Z
Boyz - Jesy Nelson, Nicki Minaj
Death Of A Bachelor – Panic! At The Disco
Here Comes The Hotstepper – Ini Kamoze
I'm Still A Guy – Brad Paisley
Macho Man – Village People
Maneater – Hall & Oates
Real Good Man – Tim McGraw
The Man – The Killers
What a Man Gotta Do - Jonas Brothers
Whatta Man – Salt-N-Pepa with En Vogue

Drama & Excitement
Another One Bites The Dust – Queen
Eye Of The Tiger – Survivor
Fever – Michael Bublé
Gonna Fly Now (Rocky Theme) – Bill Conti
Jaws Theme – John Williams
Jeopardy Theme – The Gamers
Lay Your Hands on Me – Bon Jovi
Mission Impossible Theme – Danny Elfman
Oh Yeah – Yello
Pink Panther Theme – Henry Mancini
The Stripper – David Rose

Funny Moment
Ain't Too Proud To Beg - The Temptations
Bad To The Bone - George Thorogood
How Bad Do You Want It - Tim McGraw
I Know What Boys Like - Waitresses
Keep Your Hands To Yourself - Georgia Satellites
Milkshake - Kelis
My Kinda Lover - Billy Squier
Sexy And I Know It - LMFAO
Shameless - Garth Brooks
Super Freak - Rick James
Super Freaky Girl - Nicki Minaj
Thong Song - Sisqo
U Can't Touch This - M.C. Hammer
Want to Want Me - Jason Derulo
Who Let The Dogs Out? - Baha Men

Upbeat & Fun
A Little Less Conversation - Elvis Presley
Beggin' – Måneskin
Can't Get Enough Of Your Love, Babe – Barry White
Come and Get Your Love – Redbone
Danger Zone - Kenny Loggins
I Like the Way You Move – Outkast feat. Sleepy Brown
I Wanna Be Your Lover – Prince
Lose Control - Teddy Swims
One Way Or Another – Blondie
Only U - Jade Moss
Pour Some Sugar On Me - Def Leppard
Right Round – Flo Rida
Sexyback - Justin Timberlake
Shivers – Ed Sheeran
Sucker – Jonas Brothers
The Way You Make Me Feel – Michael Jackson
You Shook Me All Night Long – AC/DC

Sexy & Risque
Body Like A Back Road - Sam Hunt
Bootylicious - Destiny's Child
Come & Get It - Selena Gomez
Earned It - The Weeknd
Hot In Herre - Nelly
I'm Too Sexy (Touch This Skin) - Black Stereo Faith
Nice & Slow - Usher
Peaches & Cream - 112
Pony - Ginuwine
Rock Your Body - Justin Timberlake
Sexual Healing - Marvin Gaye
shut up - Greyson Chance
Spicy Margarita - Jason Derulo, Michael Buble
Take You Down - Chris Brown
Toxic Pony - ALTÉGO, Britney Spears & Ginuwine
Under the Influence - Chris Brown
You Put a Spell on Me - Austin Giorgio
You Sexy Thing - Hot Chocolate

Naughty
34+35 - Ariana Grande
Anywhere - 112
Beg For It - Iggy Azalea
Cherry Pie - Warrant
Filthy - Justin Timberlake
Get Lucky - Daft Punk feat. Pharrell Williams
I Just Want to Make Love to You - Etta James
I'll Make Love to You - Boyz II Men
I'm a Slave 4 U - Britney Spears
Knockin' Boots - Luke Bryan
Let's Get It On - Marvin Gaye
Lobby - Anitta x Missy Elliott
Please Me - Bruno Mars ft. Cardi B
Slow Hands - Niall Horan
Sweetest Pie - Megan Thee Stallion and Dua Lipa
WAP - Cardi B feat. Megan Thee Stallion

Join the Wedding MusicLetter for the latest and trending wedding songs - every Wednesday.

GARTER TOSS SONGS

Upbeat & Fun
A Little Less Conversation - Elvis Presley
Get Low - Lil Jon & the East Side Boyz, Ying Yang Twins
Hey Ya! - Outkast
I Like It, I Love It - Tim McGraw
Ice Ice Baby - Vanilla Ice
It's Raining Men - Weather Girls
Livin' La Vida Loca - Ricky Martin
Party Up (Up in Here) - DMX
Right Round - Flo Rida
Save a Horse (Ride a Cowboy) - Big & Rich
Sexy And I Know It - LMFAO
Sexyback - Justin Timberlake
Shape of You - Ed Sheeran
Stayin' Alive - Bee Gees
Stray Cat Strut - The Stray Cats
Tequila - The Champs
Toxic Las Vegas (Jamieson Shaw Remix) - Elvis, B. Spears
You Sexy Thing - Hot Chocolate
You Shook Me All Night Long - AC/DC

Funny Moment
Bad To The Bone - George Thorogood
Death Of A Bachelor - Panic! At The Disco
Honky Tonk Badonkadonk - Trace Adkins
I'm Single - Jake Paul
I'm Too Sexy - Right Said Fred
Just A Gigolo - David Lee Roth
Ridin' Solo - Jason Derulo
Still Not A Player - Big Pun feat. Joe
The Way You Make Me Feel - Michael Jackson
U Can't Touch This - M.C. Hammer
Whip It - Devo
Who Let The Dogs Out? - Baha Men

I'm the Greatest
Big Pimpin' - Jay-Z
Born To Be Wild - Steppenwolf
Started From the Bottom - Drake
Way 2 Sexy - Drake feat. Future & Young Thug
We Are The Champions - Queen

All About Boys
Bad Boys - Inner Circle
Bad Boys Running Wild - Scorpions
Boys Are Back In Town - Thin Lizzy
Boys Round Here - Blake Shelton, Pistol Annies & Friends
Boyz - Jesy Nelson, Nicki Minaj
Dukes Of Hazzard Theme (Good Ol' Boys) - W. Jennings
Good Ol' Boys - Hayden Coffman
I Know What Boys Like - The Waitresses
Tall Boys - Alexandra Kay
The Boys Of Summer - Don Henley
The Wild Boys - Duran Duran

Guys Seeking Partners
Animals - Maroon 5
Blurred Lines - Robin Thicke feat. Pharrell Williams & T.I.
Bootylicious - Destiny's Child
Candy Shop - 50 Cent featuring Olivia
Get Lucky - Daft Punk feat. Pharrell Williams
Heat - Chris Brown feat. Gunna
Hot In Herre - Nelly
I Wanna Love You - Akon feat. Snoop Dogg
It's Gonna Be Me - *Nsync
Love in This Club - Usher feat. Young Jeezy
Love Sex Magic - Ciara feat. Justin Timberlake
Pony - Ginuwine
Pour Some Sugar On Me - Def Leppard
Promiscuous - Nelly Furtado feat. Timbaland
Smooth Operator - Sade
Suga Suga - Baby Bash
Suit & Tie - Justin Timberlake feat. Jay-Z
Talk Dirty - Jason Derulo feat. 2 Chainz
Talk Dirty To Me - Poison
Titi Me Pregunto - Bad Bunny
Whatever You Like - T.I.

Let's Get Ready to Rumble
Another One Bites The Dust - Queen
Back In Black - AC/DC
Bodies - Drowning Pool
Dirrty - Christina Aguilera feat. Redman
Enter Sandman - Metallica
Eye Of The Tiger - Survivor
Gonna Fly Now (Rocky Theme) - Bill Conti
Hit Me With Your Best Shot - Pat Benatar
James Bond Theme - The London Symphony Orchestra
Lose Yourself - Eminem
Mission Impossible Theme - Danny Elfman
Oh Yeah - Yello
One Way Or Another - Blondie
Pink Panther Theme - Henry Mancini
The Final Countdown - Europe
The Imperial March (Darth Vader's Theme) - John Williams
Toss It Up - 2Pac

All About Men
Fireman - Lil Wayne
Good Man - Angie Stone
Here Comes The Hotstepper - Ini Kamoze
I'm Still a Guy - Brad Paisley
Macho Man - Village People
Men In Black - Will Smith
Pretty Fly For A White Guy - Offspring
Real Good Man - Tim McGraw
Sharp Dressed Man - ZZ Top
Soul Man - Blues Brothers
The Man - The Killers
The Man - Aloe Blacc
Whatta Man - Salt-N-Pepa with En Vogue

GARTER PLACEMENT SONGS

Classic & Romantic
At Last – Etta James
Do I – Luke Bryan
Heaven – Bryan Adams
Luck Be A Lady - Frank Sinatra
Sunflower – Post Malone & Swae Lee
What Makes You Beautiful – One Direction

About a Woman
American Woman – Lenny Kravitz
Brick House – The Commodores
Country Girl (Shake It For Me) – Luke Bryan
Dangerous Woman – Ariana Grande
Foxy Lady – Jimi Hendrix
Hot Legs – Rod Stewart
Hot Mama – Trace Adkins
Legs – ZZ Top
She's A Lady – Tom Jones
Single Ladies (Put A Ring On It) – Beyonce

About a Man
Ain't No Other Man – Christina Aguilera
Big Pimpin' – Jay-Z
Death Of A Bachelor - Panic! At The Disco
Here Comes The Hotstepper – Ini Kamoze
Macho Man – Village People
Real Good Man – Tim McGraw
Single Saturday Night - Cole Swindell
Some Guys Have All The Luck – Rod Stewart
Still Not A Player – Big Punisher feat. Joe
What a Man Gotta Do - Jonas Brothers
Whatta Man – Salt-N-Pepa with En Vogue
Who Let The Dogs Out? – Baha Men
Womanizer – Britney Spears

Drama & Excitement
Another One Bites The Dust – Queen
Eye Of The Tiger – Survivor
Fever – Peggy Lee
Gonna Fly Now (Rocky Theme) – Bill Conti
Main Title (Theme From Jaws) – John Williams
Mission Impossible Theme – Danny Elfman
Oh Yeah – Yello
Pink Panther Theme – Henry Mancini
Raiders March – John Williams
The Stripper – David Rose

Sexy & Risque
Body Like A Back Road – Sam Hunt
Boombastic – Shaggy
Bootylicious – Destiny's Child
Da Ya Think I'm Sexy? – Rod Stewart
I Want Candy – Bow Wow Wow
Kiss – Prince
Pony - Ginuwine
Wild Thing – The Troggs
Wild Thoughts – DJ Khaled feat. Rihanna & Bryson Tiller
You Sexy Thing – Hot Chocolate

Funny Moment
Beggin' - Måneskin
Centerfold - The J. Geils Band
Come & Get It – Selena Gomez
Feels like the First Time – Foreigner
Hot For Teacher – Van Halen
Keep Your Hands To Yourself – Georgia Satellites
Ridin' Solo – Jason Derulo
Shameless – Garth Brooks
Super Freak – Rick James
Super Freaky Girl - Nicki Minaj
The Wanderer – Dion
Twilight Zone – Golden Earring
U Can't Touch This – M.C. Hammer

Upbeat & Fun
A Little Less Conversation - Elvis Presley
Bad To The Bone – George Thorogood
Big Energy - Latto
Born To Be Wild – Steppenwolf
Can't Get Enough Of Your Love, Babe – Barry White
Come And Get Your Love - Redbone
Danger Zone – Kenny Loggins
Drunk in Love – Beyoncé
Hey Ya! – Outkast
I Gotta Feeling – Black Eyed Peas
I'm Too Sexy – Right Said Fred
Lose Control - Teddy Swims
Nice to Meet Ya - Meghan Trainor, Nicki Minaj
Pour Some Sugar On Me – Def Leppard
Sexy And I Know It – LMFAO
Sexyback – Justin Timberlake
Start Me Up – by The Rolling Stones
Suit & Tie – Justin Timberlake feat. Jay Z
The Way You Make Me Feel – Michael Jackson
We Should Be Friends – Miranda Lambert
You Shook Me All Night Long – AC/DC

Naughty
Dirrty – Christina Aguilera feat. Redman
Earned It – The Weeknd
Filthy – Justin Timberlake
Get Lucky - Daft Punk, Pharrell Williams
Gimme All Your Lovin' – ZZ Top
Hot In Herre - Nelly
Hungry Eyes – Eric Carmen
Let's Get It On – Marvin Gaye
Lobby - Anitta x Missy Elliott
Rock Your Body – Justin Timberlake
Sexual Healing – Marvin Gaye
shut up - Greyson Chance
Slow Hands – Niall Horan
Sweetest Pie - Dua Lipa, Megan Thee Stallion
Versace On The Floor – Bruno Mars
Yummy - Justin Bieber

Join the Wedding MusicLetter for the latest and trending wedding songs - every Wednesday.

PARTY SONGS

Vibe Setting
After Hours - Kehlani
Beautiful Things - Benson Boone
BIRDS OF A FEATHER - Billie Eilish
Calm Down - Rema, Selena Gomez
Espresso - Sabrina Carpenter
Fast Car - Luke Combs
Flowers - Miley Cyrus
GOOD DAY - Forrest Frank
Move - Adam Port
Paint the Town Red - Doja Cat
Stumblin' In - CYRIL

Party Starters
A Bar Song (Tipsy) - Shaboozey
Ain't No Mountain High Enough - M. Gaye & T. Terrell
Bye Bye Bye - *NSYNC
Dance The Night - Dua Lipa
Dancing Queen - ABBA
I Wanna Dance with Somebody - Whitney Houston
I'll Be Around - The Spinners
Isn't She Lovely - Stevie Wonder
Let the Music Play - Shannon
Lil Boo Thang - Paul Russell
My Girl - The Temptations
Party In the U.S.A. - Miley Cyrus
September - Earth, Wind & Fire
This Will Be (An Everlasting Love) - Natalie Cole
Unwritten - Natasha Bedingfield
Uptown Girl - Billy Joel
Your Love - The Outfield
You're the First, The Last, My Everything - Barry White

Dancing For Everyone
All Star - Smash Mouth
Another Night - Real McCoy
As It Was - Harry Styles
Austin (Boots Stop Workin') - Dasha
Be My Lover - La Bouche
Blank Space - Taylor Swift
Came Here For Love - Sigala & Ella Eyre
Chula - Grupo Firme & Demi Lovato
Clarity - Zedd feat. Foxes
Cooler Than Me - Mike Posner
Danza Kuduro - Don Omar feat. Lucenzo
Don't Stop The Music - Rihanna
Drunk (And I Don't Wanna Go Home) - King & Lambert
Everytime We Touch - Cascada
Family Affair - Mary J. Blige
Forever - Chris Brown
Friday (Dopamine Re-Edit) - Riton, Nightcrawlers
Gasolina (Dj Buddha Remix) - Daddy Yankee
Get Down On It - Kool & The Gang
Gonna Make You Sweat (Everybody Dance Now) - C+C Music Factory

Head & Heart - Joel Corry feat. MNEK
High Hopes - Panic! At the Disco
I Don't Want To Wait - David Guetta, OneRepublic
I Had Some Help - Post Malone, Morgan Wallen
I'm Good (Blue) - David Guetta, Bebe Rexha
Jerusalema - Master KG feat. Nomcebo Zikode
Let's Groove - Earth, Wind & Fire
Miles On It - Marshmello & Kane Brown
Murder On the Dancefloor - Sophie Ellis-Bextor
Music Sounds Better With You - Stardust
My Own Worst Enemy - Lit
One More Time - Daft Punk
Pepas - Farruko
Return of the Mack - Mark Morrison
Ride Wit Me - Nelly feat. City Spud
Shake It Off (Taylor's Version) - Taylor Swift
Shivers - Ed Sheeran
Si Antes Te Hubiera Conocido - KAROL G
Sunshine (My Girl) - Wuki
The Nights - Avicii
The Way I Are - Timbaland feat. Keri Hilson & D.O.E.
This Is What You Came For - Calvin Harris & Rihanna
Thunderstruck - AC/DC
Timber - Pitbull & Kesha
Titanium - David Guetta feat. Sia
Whoomp! There It Is - Tag Team
Word Up! - Cameo
Yeah! - USHER feat. Lil Jon & Ludacris

Younger Crowd
360 - Charli XCX
Basket Case - Green Day
Blow the Whistle - Too $hort
California Love - 2Pac feat. Roger Troutman & Dr. Dre
Candy Shop - 50 Cent
Freaks - Surf Curse
Goodies - Ciara feat. Petey Pablo
HOT TO GO! - Chappell Roan
Jump Around - House of Pain
Loving On Me - Jack Harlow
MILLION DOLLAR BABY - Tommy Richman
No Diggity - Blackstreet
No Scrubs - TLC
Not Like Us - Kendrick Lamar
Pony - Ginuwine
rockstar - Post Malone feat. 21 Savage
Sandstorm - Darude
Shake Dat Ass (Twerk Song) - Bossman Dlow
The Next Episode - Dr. Dre feat. Snoop Dogg
The Show Goes On - Lupe Fiasco
Too Close - Next
We Fly High - Jim Jones
Welcome to the Black Parade - My Chemical Romance

SLOW DANCE SONGS

Classic
(Sittin' On) the Dock of the Bay - Otis Redding
A Love Song - Dazz Band
Ain't No Sunshine - Bill Withers
Bring It On Home to Me - Sam Cooke
Can We Talk - Tevin Campbell
Can't Help Falling In Love - Elvis Presley
Faithfully - Journey
Forever Young - Alphaville
How Deep Is Your Love - Bee Gees
I Want to Know What Love Is - Foreigner
I Will Always Love You - Whitney Houston
Iris - The Goo Goo Dolls
It's A Great Day To Be Alive - Travis Tritt
Just the Way You Are - Billy Joel
Landslide - Fleetwood Mac
Lean On Me - Bill Withers
Lovin' You - Minnie Riperton
My Girl - The Temptations
Nothing's Gonna Stop Us Now - Starship
So Amazing - Luther Vandross
Stand By Me - Ben E. King
Stuck On You - Lionel Richie
Unchained Melody - The Righteous Brothers
Valentine - Jim Brickman & Martina McBride
Vienna - Billy Joel
What You Won't Do for Love - Bobby Caldwell
You Send Me - Sam Cooke

Modern
Die For You Remix - The Weeknd, Araina Grande
Die With A Smile - Lady Gaga & Bruno Mars
Fantasmas - Humbe
In Your Love - Tyler Childers
Leave the Door Open - Silk Sonic
Lover - Taylor Swift
Millionaire - Chris Stapleton
Paradise - Justin Timberlake feat. *Nsync
Simply Beautiful - Maxwell
Space in My Heart - E. Iglesias & M. Lambert
Thank God - Kane Brown, Katelyn Brown
Under the Influence - Chris Brown
Until I Found You - S. Sanchez, Em Beihold
You - Eric Roberson

Indie
All I Want Is You - The Decemberists
Chasing Cars - Snow Patrol
Dandelions - Ruth B.
I Get to Love You - Ruelle
I Love You So - The Waiters
I Wanna Be Yours - Artic Monkeys
The Night We Met - Lord Huron
What's Up? - 4 Non Blondes

Romantic
All My Life - K-Ci & JoJo
All of Me - John Legend
All Your'n - Tyler Childers
Beautiful Crazy - Luke Combs
Fallin' - Alicia Keys
Gonna Love You - Parmalee
Heaven - Bryan Adams
I Choose You - Forest Blakk
I Do (Whatcha Say Boo) - Jon B.
I Love You - Climax Blues Band
If I Ain't Got You - Alicia Keys
Joy of My Life - Chris Stapleton
Let's Get It On - Marvin Gaye
Life With You - Kelsey Hart
Like I'm Gonna Lose You - Meghan Trainor, John Legend
Made For Me - Muni Long
Nobody But You - Blake Shelton, Gwen Stefani
On My Way to You - Cody Johnson
Perfect - Ed Sheeran
Spin You Around (1/24) - Morgan Wallen
Tennessee Whiskey - Chris Stapleton
Thinking Out Loud - Ed Sheeran
Yellow - Coldplay
You Are the Best Thing - Ray LaMontagne
You Are The Reason - Calum Scott

Unique
Bloom - The Paper Kites
Fade into You - Mazzy Star
Good Riddance (Time of Your Life) - Green Day
Here Without You - 3 Doors Down
I Hope You Dance - Lee Ann Womack
I'm with You - Avril Lavigne
Kiss from a Rose - Seal
Kiss Of Life - Sade
Nothing Compares 2 U - Sinéad O'Connor
Nothing Else Matters - Metallica
One In A Million - Aaliyah
Save Me - Jelly Roll, Lainey Wilson)
Sure Thing - Miguel
The Reason - Hoobastank
The Scientist - Coldplay
Under the Bridge - Red Hot Chili Peppers
With Arms Wide Open - Creed

Join the Wedding MusicLetter for the latest and trending wedding songs - every Wednesday.

MONEY DANCE SONGS

Slow to Enjoy the Moment
A Thousand Years - Christina Perri
All My Life - K-Ci & JoJo
All Of Me - John Legend
Amazed - Lonestar
Back At One - Brian McKnight
Beautiful Crazy - Luke Combs
Butterflies - Kacey Musgraves
Can You Feel The Love - Elton John
Come Away With Me - Norah Jones
Could I Love You Any More - R. Dominique, J. Mraz
Country Gold - Anne Wilson, Jordan Davis
Die A Happy Man - Thomas Rhett
End of the Road - Boyz II Men
Enough - Fantasia
(Everything I Do) I Do It For You - Bryan Adams
Faithfully - Journey
Falling Like The Stars - James Arthur
God Gave Me You - Blake Shelton
Heaven - Bryan Adams
Heaven - Kane Brown
Home - Johnny Gill, Kevon Edmonds
How Deep Is Your Love - Bee Gees
I Cross My Heart - George Strait
I Don't Dance - Lee Brice
I Don't Want To Miss A Thing - Aerosmith
I Hope You Dance - Lee Ann Womack
I Will Always Love You - Whitney Houston
I'll Be - Edwin McCain
I'll Be There - Jackson 5
I'll Be There - Mariah Carey
Incredible - James Tw
Like I'm Gonna Lose You - M. Trainor, J. Legend
Lost In This Moment - Big & Rich
Make You Feel My Love - Adele
My First Love - Avant feat. KeKe Wyatt
My Wish - Rascal Flatts
Perfect - Ed Sheeran
She's Everything - Brad Paisley
Speechless - Dan + Shay
Tennessee Whiskey - Chris Stapleton
Thank God - Kane Brown & Katelyn Brown
Thankful - Surfaces
Thinking Out Loud - Ed Sheeran
This I Promise You - N Sync
Through The Years - Kenny Rogers
Truly Madly Deeply - Savage Garden
WHAT I HAVE - Kelsea Ballerini
Whatever It Is - Zac Brown Band
Why Don't We Just Dance - Josh Turner

Fun & Upbeat
24K Magic - Bruno Mars
Brown Eyed Girl - Van Morrison
Bust A Move - Young MC
Fins - Jimmy Buffett
How Sweet It Is (To Be Loved By You) - James Taylor
I Wanna Dance with Somebody - Whitney Houston
Is This Love - Bob Marley
Isn't She Lovely - Stevie Wonder
Marry You - Bruno Mars
My Girl - The Temptations
Party In The U.S.A. - Miley Cyrus
Suavemente - Elvis Crespo
Sugar, Sugar - The Archies

Classic Hits
At Last - Etta James
Can't Help Falling In Love - Elvis Presley
Count On Me - Whitney Houston, CeCe Winans
Dancing In The Moonlight - King Harvest
I Got You Babe - Sonny & Cher
L-O-V-E - Nat King Cole
Peaceful Easy Feeling - Eagles
Stand By Me - Ben E. King
That's Amore - Dean Martin
The Way You Look Tonight - Frank Sinatra
Unchained Melody - The Righteous Brothers
What A Wonderful World - Louis Armstrong
Wonderful Tonight - Eric Clapton

About Family & Friends
Bless The Broken Road - Rascal Flatts
Buy Dirt - Jordan Davis, Luke Bryan
Doing Life With Me - Eric Church
Friends - Michael W. Smith
Friends In Low Places - Garth Brooks
From The Ground Up - Dan + Shay
Humble And Kind - Tim McGraw
Most People Are Good - Luke Bryan
Raised Up Right - Riley Green
Rich Man - Little Big Town
With A Little Help From My Friends - The Beatles
You've Got A Friend - James Taylor

All About Money
Billionaire - Travie McCoy, Bruno Mars
I Need A Dollar - Aloe Blacc
If I Had $1,000,000 - Barenaked Ladies
Millionaire - Chris Stapleton
Money - Pink Floyd
Money - Young Thug, Juice WRLD, Nicki Minaj
Money (That's What I Want) - Barrett Strong
Money Maker - Ludacris, Pharrell
No Tengo Dinero - Juan Gabriel
Rich Girl - Daryl Hall & John Oates
Rich Girl - Gwen Stefani, Eve
Ring Pop - Jax

LINE DANCE SONGS

Family Cookout
Apache – Sugarhill Gang
Bikers Shuffle – Big Mucci
Birthday Slide – Big Mucci
C'mon N' Ride It (The Train) – Quad City DJ's
Can't Get Enough – Tamia
Cha Cha Slide – Mr. C (DJ Casper)
Crank That – Soulja Boy Tell 'Em
Cupid Shuffle – Cupid
Da' Butt – E.U.
Eazy Shuffle – Eric Bellinger
Flex - Cupid
Freak It - Lathun
Harlem Shake – Baauer
Hit the Quan – iLoveMemphis
In My Feelings – Drake
Kwang Wit It - Khia
Planet Rock – Afrika Bambaataa & The Soul Sonic Force
Real Hips 2 – Defiant Presents, Dj Sliink & Bandmanrill
Same Ole 2step – Ent Distrikt
Savage – Megan Thee Stallion
Stanky Legg – GS Boyz
Step and Stomp – J Dallas
Teach Me How to Dougie – Cali Swag District
The Bird – Morris Day and The Time
The Mississippi Step – Mr. Sipp
The Zydeco Bounce – T.K. Soul
Walk It Out – Unk
Watch Me (Whip / Nae Nae) – Silentó

Made for Dances
5, 6, 7, 8 – Steps
Conga – Miami Sound Machine & Gloria Estefan
Electric Boogie – Marcia Griffiths
Electric Boogie - Shaggy, Marcia Griffiths
Footloose – Kenny Loggins
Macarena – Los Del Rio
Shout (Part I & II) – The Isley Brothers
The Git Up – Blanco Brown
The Hustle – Van McCoy
The Loco-motion – Grand Funk Railroad
The Loco-Motion – Little Eva
The Twist – Chubby Checker
The Wedding Horah – Vicki DeLor
Thriller – Michael Jackson
Time Warp – Rocky Horror Picture Show Cast
Todo, Todo, Todo – Daniela Romo
Toosie Slide – Drake
Tootsee Roll – 69 Boyz
Trucker's Slide - Arthur Young
Turbo Hustle – DJ Maestro
Twist & Shout – The Beatles
Wobble – V.I.C.
Y.M.C.A. - Village People

Just for Kids
Baby Shark – Pinkfong
Bunny Hop – Ray Anthony
Chicken Dance/Bird Dance – The Emeralds
The Hokey Pokey – Ray Anthony

Boots Kickin'
Achy Breaky Heart – Billy Ray Cyrus
Any Man of Mine – Shania Twain
Baby Likes to Rock It – The Tractors
Boot Scootin' Boogie – Brooks & Dunn
Chattahoochee – Alan Jackson
Copperhead Road – Steve Earle
Cotton Eye Joe – Rednex
Country Girl (Shake It For Me) – Luke Bryan
Country Steppin' (Remix) – JoelPatrick feat. Bryson Gray
Dancin' In The Country - Tyler Hubbard
Do the Lasso – Justin Champagne
Fancy Like – Walker Hayes
Giddy Up! - Shania Twain
Good Time – Alan Jackson
Honky Tonk Badonkadonk – Trace Adkins
I'm From The Country – Tracy Byrd
It Ain't My Fault - Brothers Osborne
Like I Love Country Music - Kane Brown
Man! I Feel Like A Woman! – Shania Twain
No Body – Blake Shelton
No Rompas Mi Corazón - Caballo Dorado
Wagon Wheel – Darius Rucker
Watermelon Crawl - Tracy Byrd
What the Cowgirls Do – Vince Gill

Party Hits
All For One - High School Musical Cast
Austin (Boots Stop Workin') - Dasha
Blurred Lines – Robin Thicke feat. T.I. & Pharrell
Burn It To The Ground - Nickelback
Chunky - Bruno Mars
Church Clap - KB, Lecrae
Goo Goo Muck – The Cramps
HOT TO GO! - Chappell Roan
Jerusalema – Master KG feat. Nomcebo Zikode
Lil Bit - Nelly, Florida Georgia Line
Limbo – Daddy Yankee
Mony Mony – Billy Idol
Old Town Road (Remix) – Lil Nas X feat. Billy Ray Cyrus
Shivers - Ed Sheeran
TEXAS HOLD 'EM - Beyoncé
We Like To Party - Vengaboys
When You Leave (Numa Numa) - Alina

Join the Wedding MusicLetter for the latest and trending wedding songs - every Wednesday.

LAST DANCE SONGS

It's Over
Bang! – AJR
Bye Bye Bye – N Sync
Carry You Home - Alex Warren
Closing Time – Semisonic
Closing Time – The Chardon Polka Band
Come Away With Me – Norah Jones
Drunk (And I Don't Wanna Go Home) – E. King, M. Lambert
Final Song - MØ
Glad You Came – The Wanted
Good Riddance (Time Of Your Life) – Green Day
Good Riddance (Time of Your Life) – R. Pope, National Parks
Happy Trails – The Avett Brothers
Hit The Road Jack – Ray Charles
Home – Edward Sharpe & The Magnetic Zeros
I Don't Want This Night To End – Luke Bryan
(I've Had) The Time Of My Life – B. Medley, J. Warnes
Incredible – James TW
It Was a Good Day – Ice Cube
Last Dance – Donna Summer
Memories – David Guetta Feat. Kid Cudi
Memories – Maroon 5
Na Na Hey Hey Kiss Hjm Goodbye – Steam
No Goodbyes (Friends Forever) - Fitz & The Tantrums
One Last Dance – John Legend
Out Of Reach – BoyWithUke
Save The Best For Last – Vanessa Williams
Save The Last Dance For Me – Michael Buble
Save the Last Dance for Me – The Drifters
Send Me On My Way – Rusted Root
Take Me Home Tonight – Eddie Money
Take Me Home, Country Roads - KSHMR
Take Me Home, Country Roads – John Denver
Young Forever – Jay-Z feat. Mr. Hudson

We're Married!
Best Day Of My Life – American Authors
Black And White – Niall Horan
Dog Days Are Over - Florence & The Machine
First Date - Blink-182
Growing Old With You - Restless Road
Here's To Us – Halestorm
Just The Two Of Us – Bill Withers, Grover Washington, Jr.
Makin' Plans – Miranda Lambert
Marry Me – Train
Marry You – Bruno Mars
The Best Is Yet To Come – Drake White
Today – Brad Paisley
Today Was A Fairytale (Taylor's Version) – Taylor Swift

Romantic
All Your'n - Tyler Childers
At Last – Etta James
Can't Help Falling In Love – Elvis Presley
Die A Happy Man – Thomas Rhett
Forever After All – Luke Combs
From The Ground Up – Dan + Shay
I Don't Want To Miss A Thing – Aerosmith
Joy Of My Life - Chris Stapleton
Love Of A Lifetime – Firehouse
Love Story – Taylor Swift
Love You Anyway – Devon Gilfillian
Perfect – Ed Sheeran
Simply the Best – Noah Reid
Stand By Me – Ben E. King
Tennessee Whiskey - Chris Stapleton
Thank God - Kane Brown & Katelyn Brown
Thinking Out Loud – Ed Sheeran
Until I Found You - Stephen Sanchez
What a Wonderful World - Louis Armstrong
Wonderful Tonight – Eric Clapton
You Are The Best Thing – Ray Lamontagne

End on a High Note
A Sky Full of Stars – Coldplay
Don't Stop Believin' – Journey
Don't Stop Believin' – Teddy Swims
Don't Stop Me Now – Queen
Firework – Katy Perry
Forever – Chris Brown
I Wanna Dance with Somebody – Whitney Houston
Miracles Happen (When You Believe) – Myra
Never Let You Go – Jason Derulo, Shouse
New York, New York – Frank Sinatra
One More Time – Daft Punk
Piano Man – Billy Joel
Stole the Show – Kygo and Parson James
Sweet Caroline – Neil Diamond
The Horses – Daryl Braithwaite
This Will Be (An Everlasting Love) – Natalie Cole
We Found Love – Rihanna, Calvin Harris

What a Party!
All The Small Things - Blink-182
Bohemian Rhapsody – Queen
Dancing In The Moonlight - King Harvest
Dancing Queen - ABBA
Friends In Low Places – Garth Brooks
Livin' On A Prayer – Bon Jovi
Mr. Brightside – The Killers
My Way – Frank Sinatra
Never Gonna Give You Up – Rick Astley
September – Earth, Wind & Fire
Unwritten - Natasha Bedingfield
We Are Family – Sister Sledge
You Shook Me All Night Long – AC/DC

PRIVATE LAST DANCE SONGS

Romance
All I See Is You - Shane Smith & The Saints
All My Life - Brooke Eden
All My Life - K-Ci & JoJo
All Your'n - Tyler Childers
Anyone - Justin Bieber
At Last - Etta James
Baby I'm Yours - Arctic Monkeys
Beautiful Crazy - Luke Combs
Best Part - Daniel Caesar, H.E.R.
Biblical - Calum Scott
Bless The Broken Road - Ally Salort
Can We Kiss Forever? - Kina
Carry You - Novo Amor
Constellations - Jade LeMac
Conversations In The Dark - John Legend
Cover Me Up - Jason Isbell
Enchanted - Talyor Swift
Falling Like The Stars - James Arthur
Find Someone Like You - Snoh Aalegra
First Date - Taylor Acorn
Growing Old With You (first dance version) - Restless Road
Heaven - Jason Aldean
I Am Yours - Andy Grammer
I Get To Love You - Lindsey Elm
I GUESS I'M IN LOVE - Clinton Kane
I'll Be - Edwin McCain
I'm With You - Vance Joy
In Case You Didn't Know - Brett Young
Let You Love Me - Jervis Campbell
Like Real People Do - Hozier
Love In Slow Motion - Ed Sheeran
More Than Me - Ian Munsick
Morning Light - The Light The Heat
Perfect - Ed Sheeran, Beyonce
Perfect For Me - Bradley Marshall
Pillows - Emanuel
Pointless - Lewis Capaldi
Still Into You First Dance Version - Isabella Kensington
Te Regalo - Carla Morrison
Thank God - Kane Brown & Katelyn Brown
That Part - Lauren Spencer Smith
The Luckiest - Ben Folds
The Night We Met - Lord Huron
This Is What Slow Dancing Feels Like - JVKE
This Town - Nathan Archie
Until I Found You - Stephen Sanchez
Valentine - Laufey
What Dreams Are Made Of - Brent Morgan
Wonderful Tonight - Eric Clapton
Wondering Why - The Red Clay Strays
Yellow - Coldplay
You & I (Nobody In The World) - John Legend
Yours Alone - Wade Bowen

New Beginning
Can't Have Mine (Find You A Girl) - Dylan Scott
Forever's As Far As I'll Go - Alabama
I Just Want To Dance With You - George Strait
I Know She Ain't Ready - Luke Combs
I Won't Give Up - Jason Mraz
Last Dance - Alfie Castley
So This Is Love - Ilene Woods, Mike Douglas
The Best Is Yet To Come - Frank Sinatra, Count Basie
The Best Is Yet To Come - Tony Bennett
This Is It - Scotty McCreery

Party's Over
Coming Home - Leon Bridges
Die With A Smile - Lady Gaga & Bruno Mars
Forever Young - Alphaville
Greatest Day Of My Life - Zach Bryan
The Party's Over - Nat King Cole
Today Was A Fairytale - Taylor Swift

A Fun Dance
Accidentally in Love - Counting Crows
Best Love Song - T-Pain
Came Here For Love - Sigala, Ella Eyre
First Date - Blink-182
Love Story - Taylor Swift
Mirrors - Justin Timberlake
The Luckiest - Josh Abbott Band
The Way - Ariana Grande, Mac Miller
Woke Up In Love - Kygo, Calum Scott

1950S WEDDING SONGS

Romantic Slow Dances
All I Have To Do Is Dream - Everly Brothers
All The Way - Frank Sinatra
April Love - Pat Boone
Autumn Leaves - Roger Williams
Chances Are - Johnny Mathis
Come Softly To Me - The Fleetwoods
Earth Angel - The Penguins
For Your Precious Love - Jerry Butler
Goodnight Sweetheart, Goodnight - The Spaniels
I Only Have Eyes For You - The Flamingos
I Walk The Line - Johnny Cash
I Want You, I Need You, I Love You - Elvis Presley
In The Still of The Night - The Five Satins
Love Is A Many-Splendored Thing - The Four Aces
Love Me Tender - Elvis Presley
My Special Angel - Bobby Helms
Only You - The Platters
Pledging My Love - Johnny Ace
Put Your Head On My Shoulder - Paul Anka
Sea Of Love - Phil Phillips
Sleep Walk - Santo and Johnny
Smoke Gets In Your Eyes - The Platters
To Know Him is To Love Him - Teddy Bears
You Send Me - Sam Cooke
Young Love - Sonny James

Classic Pop Ballads
Diana - Paul Anka
He's Got The Whole World In His Hands - L. London
It's All in The Game - Tommy Edwards
Kisses Sweeter Than Wine - Jimmie Rodgers
Little Star - The Elegants
Memories Are Made Of This - Dean Martin
Sincerely - The Moonglows
Tammy - Debbie Reynolds
Venus - Frankie Avalon
Volare - Dean Martin

Classic Rock & Roll
At My Front Door (Crazy Little Mama) - El Dorados
Blueberry Hill - Fats Domino
Bo Diddley - Bo Diddley
Honky Tonk, Part 1 - Bill Doggett
I've Got A Woman - Ray Charles
Jim Dandy - Lavern Baker
Keep A Knockin' - Little Richard
Money (That's What I Want) - Barrett Strong
Rebel Rouser - Duane Eddy
Roll Over Beethoven - Chuck Berry
Searchin' - The Coasters
The Stroll - The Diamonds
Rockin' Pneumonia & the Boogie Woogie Flu - H. Smith
Tequila - The Champs
That'll Be The Day - Buddy Holly & the Crickets

Upbeat and Fun
All Shook Up - Elvis Presley
At The Hop - Danny & the Juniors
Banana Boat Song - Harry Belafonte
Be-Bop-A-Lula - Gene Vincent & the Bluecaps
Blue Suede Shoes - Elvis Presley
Chantilly Lace - Big Bopper
Come Go With Me - The Del-Vikings
Dance With Me - The Drifters
Do You Want To Dance - Bobby Freeman
Don't Be Cruel - Elvis Presley
Gee - The Crows
Good Golly, Miss Molly - Little Richard
Great Balls Of Fire - Jerry Lee Lewis
Hang Up My Rock And Roll Shoes - Chuck Willis
Hey Good Lookin' - Hank Williams
Hound Dog - Elvis Presley
Jailhouse Rock - Elvis Presley
Johnny B Goode - Chuck Berry
Kansas City - Wilbert Harrison
La Bamba - Ritchie Valens
Let The Good Times Roll - Shirley & Lee
Little Bitty Pretty One - Thurston Harris
Little Darlin' - The Diamonds
Lollipop - The Chordettes
Love Potion No. 9 - The Clovers
Mack The Knife - Bobby Darin
Party Doll - Buddy Knox
Peggy Sue - Buddy Holly & the Crickets
Rave On - Buddy Holly & the Crickets
Rock And Roll Music - Chuck Berry
Rock Around The Clock - Bill Haley & His Comets
Rockin' Robin - Bobby Day
Sea Cruise - Frankie Ford
Sh-Boom - The Chords
Shout - The Isley Brothers
Splish Splash - Bobby Darin
Summertime Blues - Eddie Cochran
Susie Q - Dale Hawkins
Tutti Frutti - Little Richard
What'd I Say - Ray Charles
Whole Lotta Shakin' Goin On - Jerry Lee Lewis
Willie & The Hand Jive - Johnny Otis

Novelty and Unique Songs
16 Candles - The Crests
Fever - Little Willie John
Love Is Strange - Mickey & Sylvia
Tweedlee Dee - LaVern Baker

Join the Wedding MusicLetter for the latest and trending wedding songs - every Wednesday.

1960S WEDDING SONGS

Romantic Ballads
At Last - Etta James
Bring It On Home To Me - Sam Cooke
Can't Help Falling In Love - Elvis Presley
Crazy - Patsy Cline
Georgia On My Mind - Ray Charles
How Sweet It Is (To Be Loved By You) - Marvin Gaye
I Got You Babe - Sonny & Cher
My Girl - The Temptations
Stand By Me - Ben E. King
Unchained Melody - The Righteous Brothers
When A Man Loves A Woman - Percy Sledge
Will You Still Love Me Tomorrow - The Shirelles
You Make Me Feel Like A Natural Woman - Aretha Franklin
You're All I Need To Get By - Marvin Gaye & Tammi Terrell
You've Lost That Lovin' Feelin' - Righteous Brothers
You've Really Got A Hold On Me - The Miracles

Classic Rock & Roll
Bad Moon Rising - Creedence Clearwater Revival
Born To Be Wild - Steppenwolf
Brown Eyed Girl - Van Morrison
Devil With A Blue Dress On - Mitch Ryder
(I Can't Get No) Satisfaction - The Rolling Stones
I Get Around - The Beach Boys
I Saw Her Standing There - The Beatles
Jumpin Jack Flash - The Rolling Stones
Louie Louie - The Kingsmen
Magic Carpet Ride - Steppenwolf
Na Na Hey Hey Kiss Him Goodbye - Steam
Oh, Pretty Woman - Roy Orbison
She Loves You - The Beatles
Wild Thing - The Troggs
Wooly Bully - Sam The Sham & The Pharaohs

Pop Hits
Blue Moon - The Marcels
Daydream Believer - The Monkees
Duke Of Earl - Gene Chandler
King Of The Road - Roger Miller
Last Kiss - J Frank Wilson & The Cavaliers
Stay - Maurice Williams & The Zodiacs
Suite: Judy Blue Eyes - Crosby, Stills & Nash
Surf City - Jan & Dean
Surfin' U.S.A. - The Beach Boys
The Lion Sleeps Tonight - The Tokens
The Loco-Motion - Little Eva
The Wanderer - Dion
Turn! Turn! Turn! - The Byrds
Walk Don't Run - The Ventures
Wipe Out - The Surfaris
Yesterday - The Beatles
Yummy Yummy Yummy - Ohio Express

Upbeat and Danceable
Ain't No Mountain High Enough - M. Gaye & T. Terrell
Ain't Too Proud To Beg - The Temptations
Be My Baby - The Ronettes
Build Me Up Buttercup - The Foundations
Can't Take My Eyes Off Of You - Frankie Valli
Chapel Of Love - The Dixie Cups
Dance To The Music - Sly & the Family Stone
Dancing In The Street - Martha & The Vandellas
Do Wah Diddy Diddy - Manfred Mann
Gimme Some Lovin' - Spencer Davis Group
Good Lovin' - The Young Rascals
Good Vibrations - The Beach Boys
Hang On Sloopy - The McCoys
I Can't Help Myself - The Four Tops
I Got You (I Feel Good) - James Brown
I Heard It Through The Grapevine - Marvin Gaye
I Want To Hold Your Hand - The Beatles
I'm A Believer - The Monkees
In The Midnight Hour - Wilson Pickett
Mony Mony - Tommy James & The Shondells
Mustang Sally - Wilson Pickett
Proud Mary - Creedence Clearwater Revival
Respect - Aretha Franklin
Runaround Sue - Dion
Runaway - Del Shannon
Save The Last Dance For Me - The Drifters
Something's Got a Hold on Me - Etta James
Sugar, Sugar - The Archies
Sweet Caroline - Neil Diamond
The Shoop Shoop Song (It's in His Kiss) - Betty Everett
The Twist - Chubby Checker
Twist And Shout - The Beatles
Under The Boardwalk - The Drifters
Uptight (Everything's Alright) - Stevie Wonder
You Really Got Me - The Kinks

Soul and Motown Classics
Baby I Need Your Loving - The Four Tops
Baby Love - The Supremes
Chain Of Fools - Aretha Franklin
He's So Fine - The Chiffons
Hit The Road Jack - Ray Charles
I Heard It Through The Grapevine - Marvin Gaye
Reach Out I'll Be There - Four Tops
Soul Man - Sam & Dave
Treat Her Right - Roy Head & The Traits
You Can't Hurry Love - The Supremes
You're My, Soul And Inspiration - Righteous Brothers

Unique and Iconic Tracks
A Whiter Shade Of Pale - Procol Harum
Green Onions - Booker T. & The MG's
Ring Of Fire - Johnny Cash
(Sittin' On) The Dock Of The Bay - Otis Redding
What A Wonderful World - Louis Armstrong

Join the Wedding MusicLetter for the latest and trending wedding songs - every Wednesday.

1970S WEDDING SONGS

Romantic Slow Dances
Always & Forever - Heatwave
Babe - Styx
Crazy Love - Poco
Dream Weaver - Gary Wright
Fooled Around And Fell In Love - Elvin Bishop
Imagine - John Lennon
I'll Be There - The Jackson 5
Just My Imagination - The Temptations
Let's Get It On - Marvin Gaye
Let's Stay Together - Al Green
Lean On Me - Bill Withers
Stairway To Heaven - Led Zeppelin
Three Times A Lady - Commodores
Wonderful Tonight - Eric Clapton
You Are The Sunshine Of My Life - Stevie Wonder
Your Song - Elton John

Upbeat Dance Hits
Dancing Queen - ABBA
December, 1963 (Oh, What A Night!) - Four Seasons
Disco Inferno - The Trammps
Get Down Tonight - KC & The Sunshine Band
Funkytown - Lipps. Inc.
Le Freak - Chic
Play That Funky Music - Wild Cherry
Rock With You - Michael Jackson
September - Earth, Wind & Fire
Stayin' Alive - Bee Gees
Still The One - Orleans
Y.M.C.A. - Village People
We Are Family - Sister Sledge
You're The One That I Want - Travolta & Newton-John

Classic Rock & Roll
All Right Now - Free
American Pie - Don McLean
Bad, Bad Leroy Brown - Jim Croce
Brown Sugar - The Rolling Stones
Crocodile Rock - Elton John
Hotel California - The Eagles
Old Time Rock & Roll - Bob Seger
Reelin' In The Years - Steely Dan
Stuck In The Middle With You - Stealers Wheel
Sweet Home Alabama - Lynyrd Skynyrd
The Boys Are Back In Town - Thin Lizzy
Walk This Way - Aerosmith
You Ain't Seen Nothin' Yet - BTO

Soul & Funk Grooves
Can't Get Enough Of Your Love, Babe - Barry White
Brick House - Commodores
Get Ready - Rare Earth
Good Times - Chic
I Will Survive - Gloria Gaynor
Lady Marmalade - Labelle
Low Rider - War
Love Train - The O'Jays
Superstition - Stevie Wonder
You Sexy Thing - Hot Chocolate

Fun & Quirky Tracks
Bang A Gong (Get It On) - T. Rex
Happy Days - Pratt & McClain
I Think I Love You - The Partridge Family
Kung Fu Fighting - Carl Douglas
Margaritaville - Jimmy Buffett
My Sharona - The Knack
Na Na Hey Hey Kiss Him Goodbye - Steam
Rhinestone Cowboy - Glen Campbell
Rock And Roll All Nite - Kiss
Saturday Night - Bay City Rollers
Spirit In The Sky - Norman Greenbaum
Take Me Home, Country Roads - John Denver
The Hustle - Van McCoy
The Loco-Motion - Grand Funk Railroad
Werewolves Of London - Warren Zevon
What I Like About You - The Romantics
Thank God I'm A Country Boy - John Denver

Dramatic & Storytelling Songs
Fire And Rain - James Taylor
Midnight Train To Georgia - Gladys Knight & The Pips
Papa Was A Rollin' Stone - The Temptations
Paradise By The Dashboard Light - Meat Loaf
The Joker - Steve Miller Band
The Most Beautiful Girl - Charlie Rich
We Are The Champions - Queen

Join the Wedding MusicLetter for the latest and trending wedding songs - every Wednesday.

1980S WEDDING SONGS

Romantic Slow Dances
Endless Love - Lionel Richie, Diana Ross
Faithfully - Journey
Forever and Ever, Amen - Randy Travis
I Want To Know What Love Is - Foreigner
Lady - Kenny Rogers
Sexual Healing - Marvin Gaye
Somebody's Baby - Jackson Browne
Sweet Child o' Mine - Guns N' Roses
The Lady In Red - Chris De Burgh
Total Eclipse Of The Heart - Bonnie Tyler
You And I - Eddie Rabbitt & Crystal Gayle
You And Me - Rockie Robbins

Upbeat Dance Hits
1999 - Prince
All Night Long (All Night) - Lionel Richie
Billie Jean - Michael Jackson
Bust A Move - Young MC
Celebration - Kool & The Gang
Come On Eileen - Dexy's Midnight Runners
Dancing In The Dark - Bruce Springsteen
Electric Boogie - Marcia Griffiths
Footloose - Kenny Loggins
Girls Just Want To Have Fun - Cyndi Lauper
I Wanna Dance With Somebody - Whitney Houston
Into the Groove - Madonna
Let's Dance - David Bowie
Let's Groove - Earth, Wind & Fire
Love Shack - The B-52's
Never Gonna Give You Up - Rick Astley
Push It - Salt 'N Pepa
Rock With You - Michael Jackson
Super Freak - Rick James
Take On Me - a-Ha
Thriller - Michael Jackson
Uptown Girl - Billy Joel
Walking on Sunshine - Katrina and the Waves
Word Up! - Cameo
You Can Call Me Al - Paul Simon
You Make My Dreams - Hall & Oates

Pop & New Wave Favorites
Africa - Toto
Electric Avenue - Eddy Grant
Everybody Have Fun Tonight - Wang Chung
Get Outta My Dreams, Get Into My Car - Billy Ocean
How Will I Know - Whitney Houston
Jump (For My Love) - The Pointer Sisters
Need You Tonight - INXS
One Thing Leads To Another - The Fixx
Red Red Wine - UB40
The Power Of Love - Huey Lewis and the News
True Blue - Madonna
You Spin Me Round (Like A Record) - Dead Or Alive
Your Love - Outfield

Rock & Roll Anthems
Another One Bites The Dust - Queen
Any Way You Want It - Journey
Back In Black - AC/DC
Crazy Little Thing Called Love - Queen
Don't Stop Believin' - Journey
Eye Of The Tiger - Survivor
I Love Rock 'N Roll - Joan Jett & the Blackhearts
Jump - Van Halen
Livin' On A Prayer - Bon Jovi
Pour Some Sugar On Me - Def Leppard
Sharp Dressed Man - ZZ Top
Summer of '69 - Bryan Adams
Sweet Dreams (Are Made of This) - Eurythmics
Take Me Home Tonight - Eddie Money
Under Pressure - Queen & David Bowie
You Shook Me All Night Long - AC/DC

Fun & Quirky Tracks
867-5309 / Jenny - Tommy Tutone
Call Me - Blondie
Centerfold - J. Geils Band
Fishin' In The Dark - Nitty Gritty Dirt Band
Flashdance…What A Feeling - Irene Cara
Hot Hot Hot - Buster Poindexter
I Melt With You - Modern English
I Ran (So Far Away) - Flock Of Seagulls
I'm Coming Out - Diana Ross
Jessie's Girl - Rick Springfield
Karma Chameleon - Culture Club
My Prerogative - Bobby Brown
Mony Mony - Billy Idol
Rock This Town - Stray Cats
Safety Dance - Men Without Hats
Wake Me Up Before You Go-Go - Wham!
Walk Like An Egyptian - The Bangles
Whip It - Devo
White Wedding - Billy Idol
Wild Thing - Tone-Loc
Working My Way Back To You - The Spinners

Party & Crowd-Pleasers
Get Down On It - Kool & The Gang
Hot Hot Hot - Buster Poindexter
It Takes Two - Rob Base & DJ E-Z Rock
Rock This Town - Stray Cats
You Dropped A Bomb On Me - The Gap Band

Join the Wedding MusicLetter for the latest and trending wedding songs - every Wednesday.

1990S WEDDING SONGS

Party Starters & Upbeat Dance Tracks
All Star – Smash Mouth
Another Night – Real McCoy
Baby Got Back – Sir Mix-A-Lot
Believe – Cher
C'mon N' Ride It (The Train) – Quad City DJ's
California Love – 2pac feat. Roger Troutman & Dr. Dre
Cotton Eye Joe – Rednex
Everybody (Backstreet's Back) – Backstreet Boys
Finally – CeCe Peniston
Gettin' Jiggy Wit It – Will Smith
Good Vibrations – Marky Mark & The Funky Bunch
Groove Is In The Heart – Deee-Lite
Hypnotize – The Notorious B.I.G.
Ice Ice Baby – Vanilla Ice
Informer – Snow
Jump – Kris Kross
Jump Around – House Of Pain
Livin' La Vida Loca – Ricky Martin
Macarena – Los Del Rio
Mambo No. 5 (a Little Bit of...) – Lou Bega
Mo Money Mo Problems – The Notorious B.I.G.
No Diggity – BLACKstreet
Return Of The Mack – Mark Morrison
Semi-Charmed Life – Third Eye Blind
Show Me Love – Robin S
Suavemente – Elvis Crespo
Tearin' Up My Heart – N Sync
The Humpty Dance – Digital Underground
This Is How We Do It – Montell Jordan
Thunderstruck – AC/DC
Tootsee Roll – 69 Boyz
U Can't Touch This – M.C. Hammer
Vogue – Madonna
What Is Love – Haddaway
Whatta Man – Salt-N-Pepa
Whoomp! (There It Is) – Tag Team

Background/Reception & Cocktail Hour Songs
All For Love – Bryan Adams, Rod Stewart & Sting
All I Wanna Do – Sheryl Crow
Everlasting Love – Gloria Estefan
Fly – Sugar Ray
How Bizarre – OMC
I Love You Always Forever – Donna Lewis
Killing Me Softly With His Song – The Fugees
Nothing Else Matters – Metallica
Only Wanna Be With You – Hootie & The Blowfish
Smooth – Santana with Rob Thomas
The Most Beautiful Girl In The World – Prince
Waterfalls – TLC
You're Makin' Me High – Toni Braxton

Romantic & Slow Dance Songs
All My Life – K-Ci & JoJo
All My Life – Linda Ronstadt with Aaron Neville
Amazed – Lonestar
Because You Loved Me – Celine Dion
Can You Feel The Love Tonight – Elton John
(Everything I Do) I Do It For You – Bryan Adams
Hero – Mariah Carey
I Cross My Heart – George Strait
I Don't Want To Miss A Thing – Aerosmith
I Have Nothing – Whitney Houston
I Knew I Loved You – Savage Garden
I Swear – All-4-One
I Will Always Love You – Whitney Houston
I'll Be – Edwin McCain
Iris – Goo Goo Dolls
It's Your Love – Tim McGraw & Faith Hill
More Than Words – Extreme
Nothing Else Matters – Metallica
On Bended Knee – Boyz II Men
The Power Of Love – Celine Dion
You – Jesse Powell & Gerald Albright

Throwback Hits & Sing-Along Classics
..Baby One More Time – Britney Spears
Achy Breaky Heart – Billy Ray Cyrus
All The Small Things – blink-182
Boot Scootin' Boogie – Brooks & Dunn
December, 1963 (Oh, What a Night) (re-release) – Four Seasons
Dreamlover – Mariah Carey
Friends In Low Places – Garth Brooks
I Want It That Way – Backstreet Boys
I'll Be There For You – The Rembrandts
I'm Gonna Be (500 Miles) – The Proclaimers
Let Me Clear My Throat – DJ Kool
Life Is A Highway – Tom Cochrane
Man! I Feel Like A Woman! – Shania Twain
MMMBop – Hanson
One Week – Barenaked Ladies
Poison – Bell Biv Devoe
Touch Me (All Night Long) – Cathy Dennis
Two Princes – Spin Doctors
Wannabe – Spice Girls

Sentimental Ballads & Closing Songs
Crash Into Me – Dave Matthews Band
From This Moment On – Shania Twain
Good Riddance (Time Of Your Life) – Green Day
Here And Now – Luther Vandross
I Can't Help Falling In Love With You – UB40
One – U2
One Sweet Day – Mariah Carey & Boyz II Men
Save The Best For Last – Vanessa Williams
You Were Meant For Me – Jewel

Join the Wedding MusicLetter for the latest and trending wedding songs - every Wednesday.

2000s WEDDING SONGS

Party Starters & Upbeat Dance Tracks
1, 2 Step – Ciara, Missy Elliott
Are You Gonna Be My Girl – Jet
Bye Bye Bye – N Sync
Cha Cha Slide – Mr. C
Chicken Fried - Zac Brown Band
Crazy In Love – Beyonce
Cupid Shuffle – Cupid
Don't Stop The Music – Rihanna
Family Affair - Mary J Blige
Fire Burning – Sean Kingston
Forever – Chris Brown
Get Busy – Sean Paul
Get Low – Lil Jon, East Side Boyz, Ying Yang Twins
Get The Party Started – P!nk
Glamorous – Fergie, Ludacris
Hey Ya! – OutKast
Hips Don't Lie – Shakira
Hot in Herre – Nelly
I Gotta Feeling – Black Eyed Peas
In Da Club – 50 Cent
Just Dance – Lady Gaga
Let It Rock – Kevin Rudolf
Let's Get It Started – Black Eyed Peas
Life Is A Highway – Rascal Flatts
Low – Flo Rida
Music – Madonna
One More Time – Daft Punk
Party In The USA – Miley Cyrus
Promiscuous – Nelly Furtado, Timbaland
Ride Wit Me - Nelly, St. Lunatics
Right Round – Flo Rida
Rock Your Body – Justin Timberlake
Save A Horse (Ride A Cowboy) – Big & Rich
Sexyback – Justin Timberlake
Shake It – Metro Station
Starry Eyed Surprise - Paul Oakenfold
Temperature – Sean Paul
The Way You Move – OutKast
Tik Tok – Ke$ha
Viva La Vida – Coldplay
Whatever You Like – T.I.
Where the Party At? – Jagged Edge, Nelly
Wobble – V.I.C.
Yeah! - Usher, Lil' Jon, Ludacris

Sentimental Ballads & Closing Songs
Come Away With Me – Norah Jones
I Hope You Dance – Lee Ann Womack
I Loved Her First – Heartland
Landslide - The Chicks
My Wish – Rascal Flatts
Save The Last Dance For Me – Michael Buble
There You'll Be – Faith Hill

Romantic & Slow Dance Songs
A Moment Like This – Kelly Clarkson
Better Together – Jack Johnson
Bless The Broken Road – Rascal Flatts
Chasing Cars – Snow Patrol
Fallin' – Alicia Keys
Halo – Beyonce
Hero – Enrique Iglesias
I'm Yours – Jason Mraz
Lost In This Moment – Big & Rich
Love Story – Taylor Swift
Lucky – Jason Mraz & Colbie Caillat
Make You Feel My Love – Adele
My Everything – 98 Degrees
No One – Alicia Keys
She's Everything – Brad Paisley
Thank God I Found You – Mariah Carey, Joe, 98°
Then – Brad Paisley
You And Me – Lifehouse
You Are The Best Thing – Ray LaMontagne

Throwback Hits & Sing-Along Classics
All Summer Long – Kid Rock
Beautiful Day – U2
Crazy – Gnarls Barkley
Down – Jay Sean, Lil Wayne
I Believe In A Thing Called Love – Darkness
Let's Get Married - Jagged Edge
Mr. Brightside – The Killers
Our Song - Taylor Swift
Single Ladies (Put A Ring On It) – Beyonce
The Sweet Escape – Gwen Stefani
Unwritten – Natasha Bedingfield
Yes! - Chad Brock
You're Beautiful – James Blunt

Background/Reception & Cocktail Hour Songs
All For You – Janet Jackson
Angel - Shaggy
Bubbly – Colbie Caillat
Daughters – John Mayer
Everything – Michael Buble
Let Me Love You - Mario
Little Wonders – Rob Thomas
Lucky – Jason Mraz & Colbie Caillat
No Air – Jordin Sparks, Chris Brown
No One – Alicia Keys
She Will Be Loved – Maroon 5
We Belong Together – Mariah Carey
With You – Chris Brown

2010S WEDDING SONGS

Upbeat Dance Tracks & Party Starters
24K Magic – Bruno Mars
Blurred Lines – Robin Thicke, Pharrell, T.I.
Body Like A Back Road – Sam Hunt
Cake By The Ocean – DNCE
Can't Feel My Face – The Weeknd
Can't Hold Us – Macklemore, Ryan Lewis, Ray Dalton
Can't Stop The Feeling! – Justin Timberlake
Cheap Thrills – Sia, Sean Paul
Club Can't Handle Me – Flo Rida, David Guetta
Country Girl (Shake It For Me) – Luke Bryan
Danza Kuduro – Don Omar, Lucenzo
Despacito – Luis Fonsi, Daddy Yankee
DJ Got Us Fallin' in Love – Usher, Pitbull
Dynamite – Taio Cruz
Feel So Close – Calvin Harris
Finesse – Bruno Mars, Cardi B
Fireball – Pitbull, John Ryan
Firework – Katy Perry
Get Lucky – Daft Punk, Pharrell Williams
Give Me Everything – Pitbull, Ne-Yo, Afrojack, Nayer
Good Feeling - Flo Rida
I Like It – Cardi B, Bad Bunny, J Balvin
I Love It – Icona Pop, Charli XCX
In My Feelings – Drake
Mi Gente - J. Balvin, Willy William
Moves Like Jagger – Maroon 5, Christina Aguilera
My House – Flo Rida
OMG – Usher, will.i.am
On The Floor – Jennifer Lopez, Pitbull
One Dance – Drake, Wizkid, Kyla
Party Rock Anthem – LMFAO
Raise Your Glass – P!NK
Sexy And I Know It – LMFAO
Shape Of You – Ed Sheeran
Shut Up And Dance – Walk The Moon
Super Bass – Nicki Minaj
Teach Me How To Dougie – Cali Swag District
That's What I Like - Bruno Mars
The Git Up – Blanco Brown
This Is What You Came For – Calvin Harris, Rihanna
Thrift Shop - Macklemore, Ryan Lewis, Wanz
Timber – Pitbull, Ke$ha
Time Of Our Lives - Pitbull, Ne-Yo
Titanium - David Guetta, Sia
Trap Queen - Fetty Wap
Turn Down For What – DJ Snake, Lil Jon
Uptown Funk – Mark Ronson, Bruno Mars
Wake Me Up! – Avicii
Want To Want Me – Jason Derulo
Watch Me – Silento
We Found Love – Rihanna, Calvin Harris
Yeah 3X – Chris Brown

Romantic & Slow Dance Songs
A Thousand Years – Christina Perri
Adorn – Miguel
All Of Me – John Legend
Beautiful Crazy – Luke Combs
From The Ground Up – Dan + Shay
God Gave Me You – Blake Shelton
Heaven – Kane Brown
I Don't Dance – Lee Brice
In Case You Didn't Know – Brett Young
Like I'm Gonna Lose You – Meghan Trainor, John Legend
Marry Me – Train
Perfect – Ed Sheeran
Tennessee Whiskey – Chris Stapleton
Thinking Out Loud – Ed Sheeran
Wanted – Hunter Hayes
You Make It Easy – Jason Aldean

Sing-Alongs & Crowd Favorites
All About That Bass – Meghan Trainor
Call Me Maybe – Carly Rae Jepsen
Cruise – Florida Georgia Line, Nelly
Drunk In Love - Beyonce, Jay Z
Gangnam Style – Psy
Handclap – Fitz & The Tantrums
Happy – Pharrell Williams
Hotline Bling – Drake
Old Town Road (Remix) – Lil Nas X, Billy Ray Cyrus
Shake It Off – Taylor Swift
Sucker – Jonas Brothers
Suit & Tie – Justin Timberlake, Jay-Z

Background/Reception & Cocktail Hour Songs
Best Day Of My Life - American Authors
Cheerleader – Omi
Closer – Chainsmokers, Halsey
Girls Like You – Maroon 5, Cardi B
Havana – Camila Cabello, Young Thug
Ho Hey – The Lumineers
Honey Bee – Blake Shelton
I Won't Give Up – Jason Mraz
Just The Way You Are – Bruno Mars
Love On Top - Beyonce
Senorita – Shawn Mendes, Camila Cabello
Something Just Like This - Chainsmokers, Coldplay
Stuck Like Glue - Sugarland
Sugar – Maroon 5

Closing Songs & Final Dance
Die A Happy Man – Thomas Rhett
I Don't Dance - Lee Brice
Marry You – Bruno Mars
Say You Won't Let Go - James Arthur
Speechless – Dan + Shay

AFROBEATS WEDDING SONGS

Cocktail Hour
All I Want Is You - Banky W, Chidinma
Bandana - Asake and Fireboy DML
Blessed - Hil St. Soul, Noel Gourdin
Bloody Samaritan - Ayra Starr
Buga (Lo Lo Lo) - Kizz Daniel and Tekno
Calm Down - Rema and Selena Gomez
Commas - Ayra Starr
Constantly - BoyPee, Brown Joel, and Hyce
Count On Me - Pj Morton & Fireboy Dml
Drogba (Joanna) - Afro B
Essence - Wizkid, Tems
Give You Love - Juls, L.A.X.
How I Feel - Yemi Alade
If - Davido
KU LO SA - A COLORS SHOW - Oxlade
Last Last - Burna Boy
Lonely at the Top - Asake
love nwantiti (ah ah ah) - CKay
Loving You - Zinoleesky
Me & U - Tems
Monalisa - Lojay, Sarz
Move - Adam Port, Stryv, Keinemusik, Orso, Malachiii
Ojuelegba - Wizkid
One Love - Flowking Stone, Adina
Paris - King Promise
People - Libianca
Rush - Ayra Starr
Soh-Soh - Odeal
Therapy - Stonebwoy
UNAVAILABLE - Davido ft. Musa Keys
UWAIE - Kapo
Water - Tyla
Who Is Your Guy? - Spyro and Tiwa Savage
Worth My While - Manny Norté, Tiana Major9...

Party Time
1 Milli - Davido
ACTIVE - Asake & Travis Scott
Alane - Wes
BENIN BOYS - Rema, Shallipopi
Chop My Money (I Don't Care) - P-Square
City Boys - Burna Boy
Cough - Becky G and Kizz Daniel
Favourite Girl - Darkoo and Rema
Feel - Davido
Fever - Wizkid
Go -Tekno
I Adore You - HUGEL, Topic, Arash feat. Daecolm
Iko Iko (My Bestie) - Justin Wellington, Small Jam
Jerusalema - Master KG Feat. Nomcebo
Kilometre - Burna Boy
Moving - Omah Lay
One & Only - Korede Bello
Pata Pata - Miriam Makeba
Peru - Fireboy DML, Ed Sheeran
Santa - Ayra Starr, Rauw Alejandro, and Rvssian
Sugarcane - Tiwa Savage
Ting Ting - A-Star
Waka Waka (This Time for Africa) - Shakira, Freshlyground
YAYO - Rema

Romantic
All My Life - Kwesta and Mawelele
Amen - Chike
back n forth - Fireboy DML, Lagbaja
Complete Me - Simi
Fallen In Love - Chidinma
For My Hand - Burna Boy, Ed Sheeran
I Do - Lasauce, Amanda Black
Jumoke - Samm Henshaw
Love Me JeJe - Tems
Love Somebody - Rotimi
No One Like You - P Square
Oh My - Fireboy Dml
Only You - Ric Hassani
Promise - Adekunle Gold, Simi
Running (To You) - Chike & Simi
Sensational - Chris Brown, ft. Davido, Lojay

Join the Wedding MusicLetter for the latest and trending wedding songs - every Wednesday.

CHRISTIAN WEDDING SONGS

Ceremony (Processional & Vows)
1,000 Miles - Mark Schultz
Always Be Yours - Scott Drury
Believe in Love - Charlie Worsham
Bless The Broken Road - Rascal Flatts
Flesh Of My Flesh - Leon Patillo
Forever - Jason Nelson
Give Me Forever (I Do) - John Tesh, James Ingram
God Made You Just for Me - Chad Lee
Holding Hands - Steve Green
Household Of Faith - Steve & Marijean Green
I Am Certain - A. Palfreeman
I Choose You - Ryann Darling
I Promise To Love You - Phipps, Winans, Whalum
Love Never Fails - Brandon Heath
NOTHING NEW (I DO) - Wedding Version - Brandon Lake
One + One - Lawson Bates, Olivia Collingsworth
The Blessing - Kari Jobe, Cody Carnes
The Marriage Prayer - John Waller
The Prayer - Josh Groban, Charlotte Church
Till The End Of Time - Seth Carpenter
Two Becoming One - Jonathan and Emily Martin
Whatever May Come - Jeremy & Adrienne Camp
When God Made You - NewSong, Natalie Grant
When I Say I Do - Matthew West
You Make Everything Beautiful - for KING & COUNTRY..
Yours Forever - Dara Maclean

Dinner/Background Music
Above All Things - Phil Keaggy
Be Alright - Evan Craft, Danny Gokey, Redimi2
Even If - MercyMe
Follow Love - FFH
For You - Michael W. Smith
God Is Able (Acoustic) - Hillsong Worship
God Is In This Story - Katy Nichole, Big Daddy Weave
Good Good Father - Chris Tomlin
Goodness of God (Live) - CeCe Winans
Gratitude - Brandon Lake
Holy Forever - Chris Tomlin
How You Love Me - Patrick Mayberry
I Just need U. - Tobymac
Let God Write the Rest - Tyler Johnson
Love Is Here - Dave Pettigrew
Love Me Like I Am - for KING & COUNTRY, J. Sparks
Love Will Be Enough For Us - Brandon Heath
Love Will Be Our Home - Susan Ashton
Right One - Chanté Moore
Sing - Chris Tomlin, Russell Dickerson, FGL
The Truth - Megan Woods
Unfailing Love - Jimmy Needham
We Can't Lose - LP

Reception (First Dance & Couple's Dance)
Fall in Love with You - Montell Fish
Give Me a Lifetime - Anthem Lights
God Gave Me You - Dave Barnes
HER - Isaac Carree
I Found Love (Cindy's Song) - BeBe & CeCe Winans
I'm in Love With You - Fred Hammond
Jesus & You - Darrin Morris Band, Holly Tucker
Symphony - Switch, Dillon Chase
The Wedding Song - Matthew Mole
Till I Found You - Phil Wickham

Parent Dances (Father-Daughter, Mother-Son Dances)
18 Summers - Matthew West
Answered Prayer - Bob Carlisle, Lisa Bevill
Beautiful - Micah Tyler
Good Hands - Kylie Morgan
Hundred More Years - Francesca Battistelli
I Will Be Here - Steven Curtis Chapman
Reckless Love - Cory Asbury
Slow Down - Nichole Nordeman

Upbeat Dance Songs (Reception Party)
Always - Forrest Frank
Good Day for Marrying You - Dave Barnes
Good God Almighty - Crowder
I Believe - Phil Wickham
Made To Love - Tobymac
Made You for Me - Johnathan Len, Brinn Black
Magnetic - Newsboys
MY GOD - Jor'dan Armstrong
My Jesus - Anne Wilson
Nothin' Sweeter - TobyMac
Shackles (Praise You) - Mary Mary
Something Beautiful - Newsboys
Something to My Heart - Joy Hanna
Take It All Back - Tauren Wells
Thank You Lord - Chris Tomlin, Thomas Rhett, FGL
That's Who I Praise - Brandon Lake
The Goodness - TobyMac, Blessing Offor
Wherever We Go - Newsboys
Witness - Jordan Feliz

Slow Dances
All My Hope - Crowder, Tauren Wells
Angel - Casting Crowns
By Heart, By Soul - Avalon, Aaron Neville
I Can Only Imagine - MercyMe
I See Jesus - Sarah James Frank
My Life, My Love, My All - Kirk Franklin
You Say - Lauren Daigle

Reception Exit
Good Day - Forrest Frank
I Love My Wife - Rufus Troutman
I'm So Blessed (Best Day Remix) - CAIN
TOGETHER - for KING & COUNTRY, T. Kelly, K. Franklin
UP! - Forrest Frank & Connor Price

CLASSIC ROCK LOVE SONGS

Ceremony Songs
All I Want Is You - U2
Crazy Love - Van Morrison
Fields Of Gold - Sting
Have I Told You Lately - Van Morrison
More Than Words - Extreme
Songbird - Fleetwood Mac
Time In A Bottle - Jim Croce

First Dance Songs
All My Love - Led Zeppelin
Always - Bon Jovi
Everything I Do I Do It For You - Bryan Adams
Faithfully - Journey
Joy of My Life - John Fogerty
Just the Way You Are - Billy Joel
Lady - Styx
Love of a Lifetime - Firehouse
Maybe I'm Amazed - Paul McCartney
Nothing Else Matters - Metallica
The Search Is Over - Survivor

Reception (Slow Dances)
Baby, I Love Your Way - Peter Frampton
Can't Fight This Feeling - REO Speedwagon
Colour My World - Chicago
Every Rose Has Its Thorn - Poison
Home Sweet Home - Mötley Crüe
Hysteria - Def Leppard
I Don't Want to Miss a Thing - Aerosmith
I Want To Know What Love Is - Foreigner
Love Of My Life - Queen
Love Song - Tesla
Love Will Keep Us Alive - Eagles
Still Loving You - Scorpions
The Air That I Breathe - The Hollies
Waiting for a Girl Like You - Foreigner
Wonderful Tonight - Eric Clapton
Your Song - Elton John

Reception (Uplifting or Mid-Tempo)
And I Love Her - The Beatles
Be My Baby - The Ronettes
Dance With Me - Orleans
Everywhere - Fleetwood Mac
Feel Like Makin' Love - Bad Company
Follow Me Follow You - Genesis
Friday I'm In Love - The Cure
God Only Knows - The Beach Boys
Jack & Diane - John Cougar
Just Like Heaven - The Cure
Love Walks In - Van Halen
Never Tear Us Apart - INXS
Something - The Beatles
Suite: Judy Blue Eyes - Crosby, Stills & Nash
To Be With You - Mr. Big
Total Eclipse Of The Heart - Bonnie Tyler
With Your Love - Jefferson Starship

Party or Dancing (High-Energy, Fun)
Crazy On You - Heart
Gimme All Your Lovin' - ZZ Top
How Sweet It Is (To Be Loved by You) - James Taylor
I Want You To Want Me - Cheap Trick
If You Want My Love - Cheap Trick
Just What I Needed - The Cars
Let My Love Open The Door - Pete Townshend
Let's Go Crazy - Prince & the Revolution
Light My Fire - The Doors
More Than a Feeling - Boston
Pride and Joy - Stevie Ray Vaughan
Roxanne - The Police
Under Pressure - Queen & David Bowie
What I Like About You - The Romantics
Whole Lotta Love' - Led Zeppelin
You Really Got Me - The Kinks

Ending the Night
Babe - Styx
Don't Dream It's Over - Crowded House
In Your Eyes - Peter Gabriel
Nothing's Gonna Stop Us Now - Starship
The Best Of My Love - Eagles
We've Got Tonight - Bob Seger
Wild Horses - The Rolling Stones
You Ain't Seen Nothing Yet - Bachman-Turner Overdrive

COUNTRY WEDDING SONGS

Ceremony Songs
10,000 Hours Piano - Dan + Shay, Justin Bieber
Always Gonna Love You - Alana Springsteen
Another (Wedding Version) - Adam Doleac
Bless The Broken Road - Rascal Flatts
Can't Help Falling in Love - Kacey Musgraves
Flower Girl (Wedding Version) - Molly Lovette
From the Ground Up - Dan + Shay
From This Moment On - Shania Twain, Bryan White
Gonna Love You - Parmalee
I Choose You - Amanda Jordan
In Case You Didn't Know - Brett Young
My Person (Wedding Version) - Spencer Crandall
Never Til Now - Ashley Cooke, Brett Young
On My Way to You - Cody Johnson
Prayed For You - Matt Stell
Speechless - Dan + Shay
The Rest of Our Lives - Drew Green
To Make You Feel My Love - Garth Brooks
Yours - Russell Dickerson

First Dance Songs
All the Way - Shane Smith & the Saints
All Your'n - Tyler Childers
Amazed - Lonestar
Beautiful Crazy - Luke Combs
Dance With You - Brett Young
Growing Old With You - Restless Road
I Cross My Heart - George Strait
I Don't Dance - Lee Brice
Joy of My Life - Chris Stapleton
Life With You - Kelsey Hart
Lost in This Moment - Big & Rich
My Best Friend - Tim McGraw
Nobody But You - Blake Shelton, Gwen Stefani
Now I Do - Bailey Taylor
Promise to Love Her - Blane Howard
Spin You Around (1/24) - Morgan Wallen
Steady Heart (Wedding Version) - Kameron Marlowe
Thank God - Kane Brown, Katelyn Brown
You (Acoustic) - Dan + Shay

Reception (Slow Dances)
Better Together - Luke Combs
Chasing After You - Ryan Hurd, Maren Morris
Could I Have This Dance - Anne Murray
Forever To Me - Cole Swindell
God Gave Me You - Blake Shelton
If It Were Up to Me - Johnny and Heidi
Made For You - Jake Owen
Millionaire - Chris Stapleton
Neon Moon - Brooks & Dunn
One Man Band - Old Dominion
Tennessee Whiskey - Chris Stapleton
Watermelon Moonshine - Lainey Wilson

Parent Dances & Family Dances
Bridesmaids - Kylie Morgan
Bridesmaids - Tyra Madison
Dirt Cheap - Cody Johnson
Humble And Kind - Tim McGraw
I Hope You Dance - Lee Ann Womack
I Loved Her First - Heartland
My Wish - Rascal Flatts
Revival - Zach Bryan
What I Got - SmithField
Yours - Post Malone

Reception (Uplifting or Mid-Tempo)
Buy Dirt - Jordan Davis, Luke Bryan
Fast Car - Luke Combs
Forever and Ever, Amen - Randy Travis
Forever to Go - Chase Rice
Found It In You - Tiera Kennedy
Greatest Love Story - LANCO
Happy Anywhere - Blake Shelton, Gwen Stefani
Just the Way - Parmalee, Blanco Brown
Last Night - Morgan Wallen
Make It Sweet - Old Dominion
Soul - Lee Brice
Whatever Forever Is - Devin Dawson

Party or Dancing
A Bar Song (Tipsy) - Shaboozey
Austin - Dasha
Baby Likes To Rock It - The Tractors
Boot Scootin' Boogie - Brooks & Dunn
Chicken Fried - Zac Brown Band
Copperhead Road - Steve Earle
Country Girl (Shake It For Me) - Luke Bryan
Dancin' In The Moonlight - Chris Lane, Lauren Alaina
Fancy Like - Walker Hayes
Friends In Low Places - Garth Brooks
Head Over Boots - Jon Pardi
House Party - Sam Hunt
I Had Some Help - Post Malone, Morgan Wallen
Little White Church - Little Big Town
Love Story - Taylor Swift
Man! I Feel Like A Woman! - Shania Twain
Miles On It - Marshmello & Kane Brown
Ring of Fire - Johnny Cash
Save a Horse (Ride a Cowboy) - Big & Rich
Sounds Like Something I'd Do - Drake Milligan
Stuck Like Glue - Sugarland
TEXAS HOLD 'EM - Beyoncé
Wagon Wheel - Darius Rucker

Ending the Night
Die A Happy Man - Thomas Rhett
Forever After All - Luke Combs
Take Me Home, Country Roads - John Denver
Today Was A Fairytale - Taylor Swift

Join the Wedding MusicLetter for the latest and trending wedding songs - every Wednesday.

DISCO WEDDING SONGS

Dance Floor Fillers
Boogie Oogie Oogie - Taste Of Honey
Boogie Shoes - KC & The Sunshine Band
Boogie Wonderland - Earth, Wind & Fire
Celebration - Kool & The Gang
Dancing Queen - ABBA
Disco Inferno - The Trammps
Funkytown - Lipps Inc.
Le Freak - Chic
September - Earth, Wind & Fire
Shake Your Booty - KC & Sun. Band
Shake Your Groove Thing - Peaches & Herb
Stayin' Alive - Bee Gees
YMCA - Village People

Romantic & Slow Dance Songs
Everlasting Love - Carl Carlton
Fresh - Kool and The Gang
Heaven Must Be Missing An Angel - Tavares
I Found My Baby - The Gap Band
If Only You Knew - Patti LaBelle
Love Hangover - Diana Ross
Love T.K.O. - Teddy Pendergrass
Thinking Of You - Sister Sledge
You'll Never Find Another Love Like Mine - Lou Rawls
You're The Reason Why - The Ebonys

Groove & Funk
Disco Gamma - Los Charly's Orchestra
Get Down Tonight - KC & The Sunshine Band
Good Times - Chic
Jive Talkin' - Bee Gees
Let's Groove - Earth Wind & Fire
Lost In Music - Sister Sledge
Movin' - Brass Construction
Nights On Broadway - Bee Gees
Play That Funky Music - Wild Cherry
Super Freak - Rick James
The Rubberband Man - The Spinners
You Dropped A Bomb On Me - The Gap Band

Love & Heartfelt Songs
Best of My Love - The Emotions
Don't Shut Me Down - ABBA
I Love The Nightlife - Alicia Bridges
Keep It Comin' Love - KC & The Sunshine Band
Love Is In The Air - John Paul Young
Love To Love You Baby - Donna Summer
Love Train - O'Jays
More Than A Woman - Bee Gees
See You When I Git There - Lou Rawls
Tell the World How I Feel About 'Cha Baby - H. Melvin
You Know How to Love Me - Phyllis Hyman
You Sexy Thing - Hot Chocolate

Classics & Anthems
A Night to Remember - Shalamar
Ain't No Stoppin' Us Now - McFadden & Whitehead
Bad Girls - Donna Summer
Dance, Dance, Dance - Chic
Don't Stop 'Til You Get Enough - Michael Jackson
Give Me the Night - George Benson
Got To Be Real - Cheryl Lynn
I'm Coming Out - Diana Ross
Last Dance - Donna Summer
MacArthur Park - Donna Summer
Mondo Disco - El Coco
Never Can Say Goodbye - Gloria Gaynor
Ring My Bell - Anita Ward
That's The Way I Like It - KC & The Sunshine Band
Upside Down - Diana Ross
We Are Family - Sister Sledge
You Should Be Dancing - Bee Gees

Fun & Novelty Tracks
B.Y.O.B. (Bring Your Own Baby) - Sister Sledge
Car Wash - Rose Royce
Copacabana - Barry Manilow
For the Love of Money - The O'Jays
Hot Stuff - Donna Summer
I Will Survive - Gloria Gaynor
It's Raining Men - Weather Girls
Kung Fu Fighting - Carl Douglas
Ladies Night - Kool & The Gang
Lady Marmalade - Patti Labelle
Macho Man - Village People
Rasputin - Boney M.
The Hustle - Van McCoy

Upbeat & Energizing Tracks
Bad Luck - Harold Melvin & The Blue Notes
Boogie Fever - The Sylvers
Can't Hide Love - Gazzara
Dance To The Music - Sly & The Family Stone
Don't Leave Me This Way - Thelma Houston
Everybody Dance - Chic
Gimme! Gimme! Gimme! - ABBA
Heaven Knows - Donna Summer, Brooklyn Dreams
I Feel Love - Donna Summer
I'm Your Boogie Man - KC And The Sunshine Band
Knock On Wood - Amii Stewart
Night Fever - Bee Gees
P.Y.T. (Pretty Young Thing) - Michael Jackson
Rock the Boat - The Hues Corporation
Shining Star - Earth Wind & Fire
T.S.O.P. (The Sound of Philadelphia) - Mfsb, Three Degrees
Take A Chance On Me - ABBA
Turn The Beat Around - Vicki Sue Robinson
You Make Me Feel (Mighty Real) - Sylvester

EDM/DANCE WEDDING SONGS I

Entrance Songs
Higher Love – Kygo & Whitney Houston
I Gotta Feeling – Black Eyed Peas
Let's Get It Started – Black Eyed Peas
Levels - Avicii
The Nights – Avicii
This Is What You Came For – Calvin Harris, Rihanna

Background
All That Really Matters – ILLENIUM, Teddy Swims
Call You Mine – Chainsmokers & Bebe Rexha
Dancing In The Moonlight – Aexcit & HILLA
Here With Me – Marshmello feat. CHVRCHES
ily (i love you baby) – Surf Mesa feat. Emilee
Kiss Me – Lucas Estrada & AJ Salvatore
Lifetime - SG Lewis
Rockabye – Clean Bandit, Sean Paul, Anne-Marie
Something Just Like This – Chainsmokers, Coldplay
Stay – Zedd & Alessia Cara
Sway My Way – R3HAB, Amy Shark
The Middle – Zedd & Maren Morris & Grey
This Girl (Kungs Vs. Cookin' On 3 Burners) - Kungs
What A Wonderful World – SOFI TUKKER
You – Regard x Troye Sivan x Tate McRae

First Dance Songs
Dance with Me – Diplo, Thomas Rhett & Young Thug
Deep In Your Love – Alok & Bebe Rexha
Follow Me – Sam Feldt, Rita Ora
Head & Heart – Joel Corry feat. MNEK
Heaven – Dj Sammy
I Found You – Cash Cash & Andy Grammer
LAST OF US – Gryffin & Rita Ora
Lasting Lover – Sigala & James Arthur
Lighter – Galantis, David Guetta, 5 Sec. Of Summer
Runaway (U & I) – Galantis
Symphony – Clean Bandit feat. Zara Larsson
The Flame (Damon Sharpe Remix) – Tina Tara
These Are The Times – Martin Garrix feat. JRM
What Would You Do? – J. Corry, D. Guetta, B. Tiller
Won't Let You Go – M. Garrix, Matisse & Sadko

Last Dance Songs
Don't Stop The Music - Rihanna
Get Lucky – Daft Punk feat. Pharrell Williams
Glad You Came – The Wanted
Midnight – Alesso feat. Liam Payne
Never Let You Go – Jason Derulo, Shouse
One More Time – Daft Punk
Stole the Show – Kygo and Parson James
Undeniable – Kygo, X Ambassadors

Party Dance Songs
10:35 – Tiësto & Tate McRae
Around the World - Daft Punk
Body - Loud Luxury feat. brando
BREAK MY SOUL - Beyoncé
Came Here For Love - Sigala & Ella Eyre
Clarity – Zedd feat. Foxes
Crazy What Love Can Do – D. Guetta x B. Hill x E. Henderson
Day N Night – Afrojack & Black V Neck & Muni Long
Don't Be Shy – Tiësto, KAROL G
Don't You Worry Child – Swedish House Mafia
Everybody Dance – Cedric Gervais & Franklin feat. Nile Rodgers
Everytime We Touch – Cascada
Friday (Dopamine Re-Edit) – Riton x Nightcrawlers
Hello - Martin Solveig & Dragonette
Hey Brother - Avicii
HISTORY – Joel Corry & Becky Hill
How Will I Know – Whitney Houston, Clean Bandit
I'm Good (Blue) – David Guetta, Bebe Rexha
Kernkraft 400 (Sport Chant Stadium Remix) - Zombie Nation
L'amour Toujours – Gigi D'Agostino
Latch – Disclosure feat. Sam Smith
Lean On – Major Lazer feat. MØ & DJ Snake
Losing It - FISHER
Love Me Now – Kygo, Zoe Wees
Music Sounds Better With You – Stardust
My Heart Goes (La Di Da) – Becky Hill & Topic
One Kiss – Calvin Harris, Dua Lipa
One More Time – Armin van Buuren feat. Maia Wright
Purple Hat – Sofi Tukker
Really Love (R3HAB Remix) – KSI feat. R3HAB
Ritual – Alan Walker
Roses (Imanbek Remix) – Saint Jhn
Safety Dance – CARSTN & TEN TONNE SKELETON
Sandstorm – Darude
Save Me Tonight – Arty
Sexy Bitch - David Guetta feat. Akon
Shake – L.L.A.M.A, Carmen DeLeon, Ne-Yo
Stars Align – R3HAB & Jolin Tsai
Stay the Night – Sigala, Talia Mar
Summer – Calvin Harris
The Business – Tiësto
The Motto – Tiesto, Ava Max
Wake Me Up – Avicii
We Found Love – Rihanna feat. Calvin Harris
Weekend (Party, Sleep, Repeat) – Mark Mendy & Paradigm
When Love Takes Over - David Guetta feat. Kelly Rowland
Woke Up in Love – Kygo, Gryffin & Calum Scott
You for Me – Sigala x Rita Ora

Join the Wedding MusicLetter for the latest and trending wedding songs - every Wednesday.

EDM/DANCE WEDDING SONGS II

Classic Dance Hits
Another Night – Real McCoy
Be My Lover - La Bouche
Cheap Thrills – Sia Feat. Sean Paul
Cotton Eye Joe – Rednex
Dynamite – Taio Cruz
Gonna Make You Sweat - C+C Music Factory
I Like to Move It - Reel 2 Real
I Love It – Icona Pop feat. Charli XCX
Just Dance – Lady Gaga
Murder On The Dancefloor - Sophie Ellis-Bextor
Pump Up The Jam – Technotronic
Rhythm Is a Dancer - Snap!
Rhythm of the Night - Corona
Shut Up and Dance - WALK THE MOON
Titanium – David Guetta feat. Sia
Walking On a Dream - Empire Of The Sun
What Do You Mean? – Justin Bieber

New Tracks DJs Need to Know
100 Lives - Jonas Blue & Eyelar
42 - Diplo, Maren Morris
A Bar Song (Tipsy) [Remix] - Shaboozey, D. Guetta
Ain't No Mountain High Enough - Cascada
All Night - IVE & Saweetie
All Night Long - Kungs, David Guetta & Izzy Bizu
Always Forever - Romy
Apple - Charli xcx
Baby Don't Hurt Me – D. Guetta, Anne-Marie, Coi Leray
Body Moving - Eliza Rose, Calvin Harris
Dance Through The Night - Gryffin, Whethan
Don't Stop (I Wanna Know) - ATB, Dopamine
Feel So Good - DJ Free & STRIKZ
Feels This Good – Sigala, Mae Muller, Caity Baser
Finally - Swedish House Mafia & Alicia Keys
Follow the Light - Armin van Buuren & Hardwell
For Life - Kygo & Zak Abel feat. Nile Rodgers
Get Lower - Steve Aoki & Lil Jon
Good For You - Dimitri Vegas, Like Mike, Goodboys
HIGHER - Nathan Dawe & Joel Corry feat. Sacha
I Adore You - HUGEL, Topic, Arash, Daecolm
I Don't Wanna Wait - David Guetta, OneRepublic

I Found You - TWOPILOTS, Brian Michael Hinds
I Like It - Alesso, Nate Smith
I'll Be There – Robin Schulz, Rita Ora
In The Dark - Armin van Buuren, David Guetta, Aldae
Live Without Love – Shouse & David Guetta
Love On You - The Magician & A-Trak feat. Griff Clawson
MAGIC - Gryffin & babyidontlikeyou
MAGNET - Gryffin, Disco Lines & MAX
Me Gustas Tu - Paolo Campidelli
More Than Yesterday – Two Friends & Russell Dickerson
Never Be Lonely - Jax Jones, Zoe Wees
Never Going Home Tonight - David Guetta & Alesso
Next To You – Loud Luxury & DVBBS feat. Kane Brown
One in a Million – Bebe Rexha, David Guetta
One On One - The Knocks, SOFI TUKKER
Padam Padam – Kylie Minogue
Praising You – Rita Ora feat. Fatboy Slim
RATATA - Skrillex, Missy Elliott & Mr. Oizo
Real Love – Martin Garrix, Lloyiso
Rest Of My Life - Jonas Blue, Sam Feldt, Endless Summer
Riptide - TWOPILOTS
Rock Your Body - Todd Terry, Lara Klart, Alexander Technique
Shiver - John Summit & HAYLA
Smile - Martin Garrix feat. Carolina Liar
Somebody - Chris Lake, FISHER, and Gotye
Stumblin' In - CYRIL
Sunshine (My Girl) – Wuki
Thank You (Not So Bad) - Dimitri Vegas & Like Mike, Tiësto
The Door (CYRIL Remix) - Teddy Swims
The Rhythm of the Night - Alesso
Thick Of It All - Alan Walker, Joe Jonas & Julia Michaels
Tonight (D.I.Y.A) - Jax Jones, Joel Corry & Jason Derulo
Under The Sun - Ella Henderson, Switch Disco, Alok
Us - Steve Aoki, Ernest
Von Dutch - Charli XCX
We Are One - 3 Are Legend, Bryn Christopher
Whatever - Kygo & Ava Max
Where You Are - John Summit & HAYLA
Wherever You Are - Martin Garrix & DubVision, Shaun Farrugia
Without You - Kygo & Ava Max
Without You – Alesso
Your Love (Diplo Remix) - The Outfield & Diplo

Join the Wedding MusicLetter for the latest and trending wedding songs - every Wednesday.

FOLK WEDDING SONGS

Ceremony Songs
All My Love - Cathartic Fall
Anything - JJ Heller
Everything to Me - Ivan & Alyosha
Forever - Ben Harper
I've Made Up My Mind to Give Myself to You - B. Dylan
Love Is - Zach Winters
Make These Colors Real - Hush Kids
Nothing Can Keep Me from You - The Sweeplings
One For Me - Mary Hopkin
Simply The Best - Billianne
Stumble Together - Matt Bednarsky
Take The World - JOHNNYSWIM
That's The Way Love Goes - H. Carll, A. Moorer
Till Death Do Us Part - Lily Hormel
Valentine's Day (Acoustic) - David Tribble
Wedding Blessing - Adelyn & Ava
Wedding Song (There Is Love) - Noel Paul Stookey
What a Wonderful World - Sawyer Fredericks
When You Love Someone (Live) - Gretchen Peters
You and I - SYML and Charlotte Lawrence
You're the One (Acoustic) - Luca Fogale

Processional Songs
Belong with You - The Light the Heat
Bride - Aria & Oaken
Chances - Fox and Bones
Forever & Back - Anders Sohn
Forever and for Always - Jarrod Morris
I Will Spend My Whole Life - Imaginary Future, Grannis
I'd Be Your Man - Parker Twomey
I'll Be with You - Matt + Abi
Marry Me - The Wicks
Rest of Our Lives - The Light the Heat
Someone Like Me (Wedding Version) - July Moon

Upbeat Cocktail Songs
Big Yellow Taxi - Joni Mitchell
Bubbly - Colbie Caillat
Fast Car - Tracy Chapman
Half of forever - Henrik
Hey Ho - The Lumineers
If I Say That I Love You - Foster
L O V E L O V E - Jeremy Lister
Meant For Me - Alisan Porter
Not Just Any Old Love Song - Luke Cerny
Only Love - Ben Howard
Simple Thing - Jonathan Wilson
Sunshine - Leucadia
Sweet Talk - Iron & Wine
Turning Onto You - First Aid Kit
Understand My Love - Brandon Mills
Until You - AHI
Where You Are - The National Parks
Wild World - Yusef/Cat Stevens
You're the One - Rhiannon Giddens

Background Music
All The Gold - Alivan Blu
Before You - Fortunate Ones
Bloom - The Paper Kites
Colors - Langhorne Slim
Forever From Now - Sheffield
Give All - Jon Danforth
Higher Love - James Vincent McMorrow
Hold You - Amos Lee
I And Love And You - The Avett Brothers
I Just Love You - Roo Panes
If I Didn't Love You - Ben Abraham
Let It Be Me - Ray LaMontagne
Lover's Lullaby - Sweet Tea Project
Lucky Star - Last Birds
One and Only - Garrett Kato
Perfect to Me - Josh Tatofi
Sea Of Love - Langhorne Slim, Jill Andrews
Soul Mate - flora cash
Steal My Heart Away - The Paper Kites, Ainslie Wills
This Beautiful Life - Ocie Elliott
Timber! - The National Parks

First Dance Songs
Better Part of Me - SYML, Sara Watkins
Dance With Me - Phillip Phillips
Easy Together - Drew Holcomb & The Neighbors
Heart's On Fire - Passenger
Helplessly I Fell - Jim Lord
Home - Josh Beeman
I Chose You - Caleb Edens
In Spite Of Ourselves - John Prine and Iris DeMent
The First Time - The Brave Collide
The Mountain Song (First Dance Version) - Tophouse
Touching Heaven - JOHNNYSWIM
You Have Stolen My Heart - Brian Fallon

Reception Dance Songs
All I Want Is You - Barry Louis Polisar
All the Ways - The Secret Sisters, Ray LaMontagne
Closer To Fine - Indigo Girls
How Sweet It Is (To Be Loved By You) - James Taylor
I Got You - Michael Franti & Spearhead
I Hope You Dance - The Hound + the Fox
I Want To Spend It With You - The Satellite Station
No Matter Where You Are - Us The Duo
Peach Fuzz - Caamp
Sweet Pea - Amos Lee
Touch of Grey - Grateful Dead

Last Dance Songs
Good Riddance - Ron Pope, The National Parks
If I Can't Take You With Me - Heather Stewart
Love You 'Till the End - The Pogues
Welcome Home - Fox and Bones
When You Say Nothing At All - Alison Krauss

HIP HOP WEDDING SONGS

Entrance Songs
All I Do Is Win - DJ Khaled
Congratulations - Post Malone feat. Quavo
I Gotta Feeling – Black Eyed Peas
Let's Get Married (ReMarqable Remix – Jagged Edge
My House – Flo Rida

First Dance Songs
Best I Ever Had – Drake
Favorite Song - Toosii
Girl Of My Dreams – Juice WRLD, Suga, BTS
I'll Be There For You… – Method Man, Mary J. Blige
Love Music – Lil Yachty

Cocktail Hour & Background Songs
All the Stars – Kendrick Lamar & SZA
Beautiful – Snoop Dogg featuring Pharrell Williams
Circles – Post Malone
Good Day – Nappy Roots
I Like You (A Happier Song) – Post Malone, Doja Cat
I'm the One – DJ Khaled
If I Ruled The World (Imagine That) - Nas, Lauryn Hill
LOVE. – Kendrick Lamar FT. ZACARI
marry me - KANII
Paint The Town Red - Doja Cat
Sunflower – Post Malone & Swae Lee

Group Dances
C'mon N' Ride It (The Train) – Quad City DJ's
Crank That (Soulja Boy) – Soulja Boy Tell 'Em
Cupid Shuffle – Cupid
Da Dip – Freak Nasty
Electric Slide (Shall We Dance) – Grandmaster Slice
Harlem Shake – Baauer
Teach Me How to Dougie – Cali Swag District
Watch Me (Whip / Nae Nae) – Silento
Wobble – V.I.C.

Classic & Old School Vibes
Apache – The Sugarhill Gang
Baby Got Back – Sir Mix-A-Lot
Bust A Move – Young MC
California Love – 2 Pac
Fantastic Voyage – Coolio
Ghetto Supastar (That is What You Are) - Pras
Hypnotize – Notorious B.I.G.
Ice Ice Baby – Vanilla Ice
It Takes Two – Rob Base & DJ E-Z Rock
It's Tricky – Run DMC
Jump Around – House Of Pain
Just a Friend – Biz Markie
Let Me Clear My Throat – DJ Kool
Nuthin' But A "G" Thang – Dr. Dre featuring Snoop Dogg
Regulate – Warren G feat. Nate Dogg
Shoop – Salt-n-Pepa
The Next Episode – Dr. Dre feat. Snoop Dogg
What You Want – Mase feat. Total
Whoomp! There It Is – Tag Team

Party Dance Songs
Best Friend – Saweetie feat. Doja Cat
Big Energy – Latto
Blow the Whistle - Too $hort
Body – Megan Thee Stallion
Bottoms Up – Trey Songz feat. Nicki Minaj
Can I Get A… – Jay-Z feat. Amil & Ja Rule
Can't Hold Us – Macklemore & Ryan Lewis feat. Ray Dalton
Cyclone – Baby Bash w/T-Pain
Day 'N' Nite (Nightmare) – Kid Cudi
Fancy – Iggy Azalea feat. Charli XCX
Feel so Good – Mase
Flex (Ooh, Ooh, Ooh) - Rich Homie Quan
Get Low – Lil Jon & The East Side Boyz & Ying Yang Twins
Good Feeling – Flo Rida
Got Your Money – Ol' Dirty Bastard feat. Kelis
Grove St. Party - Waka Flocka Flame feat. Kebo Gotti
Hey Ya! – Outkast
HUMBLE. - Kendrick Lamar
I Just Wanna Love U (Give It 2 Me) – Jay-Z
I Like It – Cardi B, Bad Bunny & J Balvin
In Da Club – 50 Cent
Kiss Me Thru The Phone – Soulja Boy Tell'em feat. Sammie
Lean Back – Terror Squad
Lip Gloss - Lil Mama
Lollipop - Lil Wayne feat. Static Major
London Bridge - Fergie
Lose Control - Missy Elliott feat. Ciara & Fat Man Scoop
Lose Yourself - Eminem
Low – Flo Rida
One Dance - Drake
Players - Coi Leray
Ride Wit Me – Nelly
Snap Yo Fingers - Lil Jon
Starships – Nicki Minaj
The Show Goes On - Lupe Fiasco
The Way I Are - Timbaland feat. Keri Hilson & D.O.E.
This Is How We Do It – Montell Jordan
Trap Queen – Fetty Wap
Turn Down For What – DJ Snake feat. Lil Jon
Up – Cardi B
We Fly High - Jim Jones
We Takin' Over - DJ Khaled
X Gon' Give It To Ya - DMX

New Tracks
Big Dawgs - Hanumankind & Kalmi
FE!N - Travis Scott feat. Playboi Carti
Get It Sexyy - Sexyy Red
Like That - Future, Metro Boomin & Kendrick Lamar
Lovin On Me - Jack Harlow
MILLION DOLLAR BABY - Tommy Richman
Neva Play - Megan Thee Stallion feat. RM of BTS
Not Like Us - Kendrick Lamar
TGIF - GloRilla

INDIE WEDDING SONGS

Prelude & Processional
Always in All Ways - AJ Raggs
Anywhere – Risk & Refuge
Bloom – The Paper Kites
Evermore – Hollow Coves
Falling Slowly – Glen Hansard and Marketa Irglova
Flightless Bird, American Mouth – Iron & Wine
I Get To Love You – Ruelle
I Only Want To Be With You – Birdy
If I Didn't Love You – Ben Abraham
It's Always Been You – Caleb Hearn
Landslide - Oh Wonder
Nobody Else - Dave Thomas Junior
Sea Of Love – Cat Power
The Best Thing – Paper Planes
The Luckiest – Ben Folds
The One – Kodaline

Recessional
Always Be Yours – Scott Drury
First Day Of My Life – Bright Eyes
Here - Tom Grennan
Home – Matthew Hall
I Will Follow You into the Dark – Death Cab for Cutie
Mine Forever - Voyageur
Overwhelmed – Tim McMorris
Side By Side – Jon Foreman, Madison Cunningham
You Are The Best Thing – Ray LaMontagne
You've Got the Love – Florence + The Machine

Cocktail Hour
Amazing – Plaid Brixx
Amazing – Rex Orange County
Baby I'm Yours – Arctic Monkeys
Baby It's You – London Grammar
Beach House - daydreamers
Bright – Echosmith
Doing to Me – Lou Sedo
Heat Waves - Glass Animals
Hypotheticals – Lake Street Dive
In My Arms – Billy Raffoul
Let It Happen - Tame Impala
Let's Get Married - Bleachers
Lost - Frank Ocean
Lost on You – LP
Loving You – Cannons
Missing Piece – Vance Joy
Only One – Phantom Planet
Stolen Dance - Milky Chance
Superposition – Young The Giant
Sweater Weather - The Neighbourhood
Sweetest Thing – Allman Brown
The Best - Nicotine Dolls
this is love – Walk Off the Earth
Why I Love You – Grentperez
You – Armaan Malik

First Dance
All My Love – George Ezra
Amazing – Teddy Swims
Amen – John Adams
Better Half of Me – Tom Walker
Fall Into Me (Acoustic) – Forest Blakk
Finally // beautiful stranger – Halsey
I Don't Know Any Better – Johnny and Heidi
I GUESS I'M IN LOVE – Clinton Kane
Made to Love You – Drew Angus
Our Song (Acoustic) – Ron Pope
The Night We Met - Lord Huron
way after forever - Vaultboy

Dinner
Baby, You Know – Ocie Elliott
Falling In Love – Cigarettes After Sex
Falling in Love at a Coffee Shop – Landon Pigg
I Was Born To Love You – Ray LaMontagne, Sierra Ferrell
I'll Be Around – Garrett Kato
I'm With You – Vance Joy
Landed - Ruelle, Aron Wright
Magnificent – Oh Wonder
My Love Will Follow You – Dave Barnes
Next to You – Michael Shynes
Northern Wind – City and Colour
Say Yes To Heaven - Lana Del Rey
Space Song - Beach House
The Way I Love You – Michal Leah
What a Wonderful World – Kina Grannis & Imaginary Future
You And I – Wilco

Last Dance
Birds of a Feather - Billie Eilish
Grow Old with Me – Tom Odell
Starburster - Fontaines D.C.
Summertime Sadness - Lana Del Rey
Wedding Song (Acoustic) – Yeah Yeah Yeahs

After Party
'Til I Found You – Jeremy Loops
Electric Love – BøRNS
Everything Now – Arcade Fire
Just You and I – Tom Walker
Love You For A Long Time – Maggie Rogers
Maps – Yeah Yeah Yeahs
Meet Me At Our Spot – THE ANXIETY & WILLOW & Tyler Cole
No One's Gonna Love You – Band of Horses
Rollercoaster - Bleachers
Stick Season - Noah Kahan
Sugar Babies – Spoon
The Adults Are Talking - The Strokes
The Great Divide – The Shins

Join the Wedding MusicLetter for the latest and trending wedding songs - every Wednesday.

INSTRUMENTAL WEDDING SONGS

Violin
10,000 Hours – ItsAMoney
All of Me – Alison Sparrow
Between Twilight – Lindsey Stirling
Can't Help Falling In Love – Daniel Jang
Canon in D – VioDance
Enchanted - Ana Done
Hallelujah – Alison Sparrow
I Will Always Love You – Josh Vietti
Jesu Joy of Mans Desiring – The Violin Sisters
Perfect – Taylor Davis
Something Just Like This – Ember Trio
The Joker and the Queen – Daniel Jang
Wedding March – Jean Louis Prima, Christen
Without You – Josh Vietti
Young and Beautiful - Ashot Dumanyan

Piano
10,000 Hours (Piano) - Dan + Shay & Justin Bieber
A Thousand Years - Riyandi Kusuma
A Sky Full Of Stars - Marlene T
A Whole New World - Disney Peaceful Piano
All Of Me - O'Neill Brothers Group
Ava Maria - Robbins Island Music Artists
Back At One - Johan Sander
God Bless the Broken Road - O'Neill Brothers Group
Here Comes the Sun - David Lanz
Hold My Hand - Alexandre Pachabezian
It's Your Day - Yiruma
Joy - George Winston
Kiss The Rain - Yiruma
Nothing Else Matters - Scott D. Davis
River Flows In You - Yiruma
The Prayer - Lorie Line
Until I Found You (Piano Version) – Stephen Sanchez
Wedding March (Here Comes the Bride) - O'Neill Brothers
Yellow - Henry Smith
You Are the Reason - The Theorist

Guitar
A Whole New World - Disney Ukulele
Dancing in the Moonlight - Billy Travers
Here Comes the Sun - Instrumental Songs Music
I Won't Give Up - O'Neill Brothers Group
I'm Yours - Guitar Tribute Players
Isn't She Lovely - Mount Hayes
Let It Be Me - Roberto Dalla Vecchia
Marry Me - United Guitar Players
Meant To Be - Steve Petrunak
What a Wonderful World - Tingstad & Rumbel
Yellow - Virgo Rising
You Are the Best Thing - Fred Turnquist
Your Song - United Guitar Players

Cello
Air on a G String - Hauser
Ashitaka and San - CelloKat
Livin' on a Prayer - 2Cellos
Moon River - 2Cellos
My Gift Is My Song - HAUSER
River Flows in You - Hauser

String Quartets & Groups
All I Want Is You - Bridesmaids Quartet
All You Need Is Love – Midnite String Quartet
Anyone – UNSECRET and Unsecret String Quartet
Beautiful Thing - Old Foes
Bittersweet Symphony - Dallas String Quartet
Brown Eyed Girl - Midnite String Quartet
Can't Help Falling in Love - Vitamin String Quartet
Disney Medley - 40 Fingers
Nothing Else Matters - Golden Salt
Stay With Me - Vitamin String Quartet
Such Great Heights - Section Quartet
The Luckiest - Benaud Trio
Watermelon Sugar - UNSECRET

Instrument Combos
A Thousand Years - The Piano Guys
A Thousand Years - VioDance
Beethoven's 5 Secrets – The Piano Guys
Bless the Broken Road - The Piano Guys
Canon in D - Brooklyn Duo
Enchanted - The Piano Guys
Feels Like Home - Bridesmaids Quartet
First Day of My Life - Brooklyn Duo
Perfect - Paul Hankinson Covers
Say You Won't Let Go (Instrumental) - Ariella Zeitlin
You Are The Reason - Piano Guys, Dallas String Quartet

TV & Film
A Thousand Years – VioDance
Beauty and the Beast – Daniel Jang
Bella's Lullaby - Stan Whitmire
Fairy Tail Theme – Taylor Davis
Game of Thrones Theme (Violin Cover) – Josh Vietti
Glasgow Love Theme - Craig Armstrong
Jurassic Park Theme – Vitamin String Quartet
Married Life - The Wild Conductor
Once Upon a Time… Storybook Love - Mark Knopfler
Parla più piano - The Speakeasies' Swing Band!
Rewrite the Stars - Piano Peace
The Lord of Rings The Fellowship of the Rings – Concerning Hobbits – Vitamin String Quartet
Turning Page (Instrumental) - Sleeping At Last
Victor's Piano Solo - Daniel Packard
Wildest Dream - Duomo

Join the Wedding MusicLetter for the latest and trending wedding songs - every Wednesday.

JAZZ WEDDING SONGS

Classic Jazz Standards & Vocals
A Sunday Kind Of Love - Etta James
At Last - Etta James
Cheek To Cheek - Tony Bennett, Lady Gaga
Come Fly with Me - Frank Sinatra
Come Rain Or Come Shine - Ray Charles
Dream A Little Dream Of Me - Fitzgerald, Armstrong
Feeling Good - Nina Simone
Fly Me To The Moon - Frank Sinatra, Count Basie
Give Me A Kiss To Build A Dream On - Louis Armstrong
I Get A Kick Out Of You - Tony Bennett & Lady Gaga
I've Got A Crush On You - Ella Fitzgerald
In the Mood - Glenn Miller and His Orchestra
Just the Two of Us - Bill Withers & Grover Washington, Jr.
L-O-V-E - Nat King Cole
Let's Do It (Let's Fall In Love) - Armstrong, Fitzgerald
Love Is Here To Stay - Tony Bennett, Diana Krall
My One and Only Love - John Coltrane, J. Hartman
My Way - Frank Sinatra
Smile - Nat King Cole
Something's Got A Hold On Me - Etta James
That's Amore - Dean Martin
The Way You Look Tonight - Frank Sinatra
Theme From New York, New York - Frank Sinatra
There Is No Greater Love - Chet Baker
Unforgettable - Nat King Cole, Natalie Cole
What A Wonderful World - Louis Armstrong
When I Fall In Love - Nat King Cole
Who Loves You? - Billie Holiday, Teddy Wilson
You Stepped Out Of A Dream - Sarah Vaughan

Pop & Mainstream
A Wink And A Smile - Harry Connick Jr.
Breezin' - George Benson
Cantaloop (Flip Fantasia) - Us3
Don't Worry Be Happy - Bobby McFerrin
Feels so Good - Chuck Mangione
Give Me the Night - George Benson
Giving You The Best That I Got - Anita Baker
Hold On - Michael Bublé
Love X Love - George Benson
Moondance - Van Morrison
On Broadway - George Benson
Recipe For Love - Harry Connick Jr.
Sea of Love - Brad Holt
Sweet Love - Anita Baker
The Best Is Yet To Come - Michael Bublé
We're in This Love Together - Al Jarreau
What You Won't Do for Love - Bobby Caldwell
You And I - Michael Bublé
Your Love is King - Sade

Smooth Jazz & Contemporary Jazz
Upbeat Tempo
Champagne of My Life - Peet Project
I Like the Way You Move - Bill McGee
Let's Face The Music And Dance - Jeff Goldblum
Lov-Lov-Love - Mario Biondi, Incognito
Lovefool - Scott Bradlee's Postmodern Jukebox
Lovely Day - José James
My Baby Just Cares For Me - Jeff Goldblum
Never Quit Loving You - Jill Barber
Rise - Herb Alpert
So in Love - Art Sherrod Jr
Soulful Strut - Grover Washington, Jr.
That's Enough - Janelle Monáe

Slow Tempo
A Song for You - Herbie Hancock feat. Christina Aguilera
All I Want Is You - Boney James feat. October London
Best Part - RJC (Rhythm & Jazz Coalition)
Better Than I Imagined - Robert Glasper
Coastin' - Boney James, Lalah Hathaway
Come Away With Me - Norah Jones
Don't Know Why - Norah Jones
Everything to Me - Imagesong
Everything You Touch Is Gold - Gregory Porter
Happy Feelings - Frankie Beverly & Maze Smooth Jazz Tribute
It Had To Be You - Jac Ross
Let's Fall In Love - Diana Krall
Our Love Is Here to Stay - C. Collins, A. Olatuja
So Emotional - Miles Davis, Lalah Hathaway
Someone Like You - Van Morrison feat. Joss Stone
That's the Way Love Goes - Norman Brown
The Nearness of You - Norah Jones

Latin Jazz
A Taste of Honey – Herb Alpert & The Tijuana Brass
Ladyfingers – Herb Alpert & The Tijuana Brass
Mais Que Nada – Sergio Mendes & Brasil '66
The Girl from Ipanema – Stan Getz & João Gilberto

Bossa Nova
From The Start - Laufey
It Could Happen To You - Laufey
Take Five - Dave Brubeck
The Look Of Love - Diana Krall
The Way You Look Tonight - Karen Souza
Valentine - Laufey

Join the Wedding MusicLetter for the latest and trending wedding songs - every Wednesday.

LATIN WEDDING SONGS

Party Songs...

Bachata
Medicina De Amor - Raulín Rodríguez
Obsesión - Aventura
Dos Locos - Monchy y Alexandra
Propuesta Indecente - Romeo Santos
Bachata en Fukuoka - Juan Luis Guerra

Salsa
Vivir Mi Vida - Marc Anthony
La vida es un carnaval - Celia Cruz
Fruko y Sus Tesos - El Preso
Rebelion - Joe Arroyo
Llorarás - Oscar D'León

Cumbia
Cumbia sampuesana - Aniceto Molina
Tao, Tao - Control
Baila Esta Cumbia - Selena
Mentirosa - Ráfaga
Tabaco Y Ron - Rodolfo y su Tipica

Merengue
La Dueña del Swing - Los Hermanos Rosario
Después de la Playa - Bad Munny
Suavemente - Elvis Crespo
Tu Eres Ajena - Eddy Herrera
No Me Digas Que No - La Makina

Latin Rock
Oye Mi Amor - Maná
Devuélveme a mi chica - Hombres G
Lamento Boliviano - Los Enanitos Verdes
Lobo-hombre en Paris- La Unión
En algún lugar - Duncan Dhu

Regional/Norteño
La Puerta Negra - Los Tigres del Norte
La Chona - Los Tucanes de Tijuana
El Sonidito - Hechizeros Band
Banda Sinaloense MS de Sergio Lizárraga - El Mechón
Zapateado Encabronado - Alacranes Musical

Reggaeton
Gasolina - Daddy Yankee
Me porto bonito - Bad Bunny, Chencho Corleone
Rakata - Wisin, Yandel
Yo Voy - Daddy Yankee, Zion, Lennox
LALA - Myke Towers

Party songs courtesy of @djdreovalle

Slow Dances
Creo en Ti - Reik
Darte un Beso - Prince Royce
fantasmas - HUMBE
No Crezcas Mas - Tercer Cielo
No Hay Nadie Más - Sebastián Yatra
Yo Quería - Cristian Castro
Yo También - Romeo Santos feat. Marc Anthony

Mexican/White First Dance Songs
Cuando Me Enamoro - Enrique Iglesias ft Juan Luis Guerra
Dos Oruguitas - Sebastián Yatra
Dreaming Of You - Selena
Forever My Love - J. Balvin, Ed Sheeran
Homesick - Kane Brown & Río Roma
Hoy Tengo Ganas De Ti - A. Fernández, C. Aguilera
I Adore Mi Amor - Color Me Badd
I Could Fall In Love - Selena
I Want It All (Spanglish Version) - Kat & Alex
Lost in the Middle of Nowhere (Spanish Remix) - K. Brown, B. G
Lucky - Jason Mraz, Ximena Sariñana
Marry Me (Ballad) - Jennifer Lopez, Maluma
My Baby You - Marc Anthony
My Only One (No Hay Nadie Más) - I. Merced, S. Yatra
Ocean (Remix) - Karol G and Jessie Reyez
Por Siempre Tú - Christina Aguilera
Space in My Heart - Enrique Iglesias, Miranda Lambert
Stand by Me - Prince Royce
We Belong Together - Los Lobos
Yo Te Voy A Amar (This I Promise You) - *NSync

Join the Wedding MusicLetter for the latest and trending wedding songs - every Wednesday.

LGBTQ+ WEDDING SONGS

First Dance & Love Songs
A Simple Love - Melissa Etheridge
Always Be My Man – Billy Porter, Luke Evans
Amazed Acoustic - Shane Filan
Angel Baby - Troye Sivan
At My Most Beautiful - R.E.M.
Biblical - Calum Scott
Can't Help Falling In Love - Kacey Musgraves
Closer - Tegan and Sara
Colour – MNEK ft. Hailee Steinfeld
Drive Me, Crazy - Orville Peck
Easy - Pale Waves
Follow Your Arrow - Kacey Musgraves
Forrest Gump - Frank Ocean
Heaven – Calum Scott
Hold Each Other - A Great Big World feat. Futuristic
I Do - Maryann and Ron Sfarzo
Imagine (Acoustic) – Ben Platt
Latch Acoustic - Sam Smith
Love is Love - Trey Pearson
Origin of Love - Mika
Our Song - Jaymes Vaughan
Parentheses - The Blow
She Keeps Me Warm - Mary Lambert
So Beautiful - Darren Hayes
Sofia - Clairo
Sweet Symphony – Joy Oladokun, Chris Stapleton
To Make You Feel My Love - Adele
What a Beautiful Day - Brett Every
You Are The Reason – Calum Scott

Parents Dance
Everything – Matthew John
In My Life – The Beatles
look up - Joy Oladokun
No Matter What – Calum Scott
So Will I - Ben Platt

Classic Party
Beautiful - Christina Aguilera
Believe - Cher
Can't Take That Away (Mariah's theme) - Mariah Carey
Dancing Queen - ABBA
Don't Stop Me Now - Queen
Finally - CeCe Peniston
Gimmie! Gimmie! Gimmie! - ABBA
I Am What I Am - Gloria Gaynor
I Kissed A Girl - Katy Perry
I Wanna Dance With Somebody - Whitney Houston
I Want To Break Free - Queen
I'm Coming Out - Diana Ross
It's Raining Men - The Weather Girls
Man! I Feel Like A Woman! - Shania Twain
Murder on the Dancefloor - Sophie Ellis-Bextor
Show Me Love - Robin S
Vogue - Madonna
Wade In The Water - Ramsey Lewis
Y.M.C.A. - Village People

Modern Party
360 - Charlie xcx
All the Lovers - Kylie Minogue
Amelie - Gracie Abrams
Because of You - Gustaph
Born This Way - Lady Gaga
Cool for the Summer - Demi Lovato
Dancing On My Own - Robyn
Gay Excellence - Todrick Hall
Girls Like Girls - Hayley Kiyoko
Girls/Girls/Boys - Panic! At The Disco
God Is A Woman - Arian Grande
Good Luck, Babe! - Chappell Roan
Hot To Go! - Chappell Roan
I Feel Love - Sam Smith
I'm Finally Me - Cast from ZOMBIES 3
(It Goes Like) Nanana - Peggy Gou
Lights Up - Harry Styles
Montero (Call Me By Your Name) - Lil Nas X
Only The Brave - Louis Tomlinson
Padam Padam - Kylie Minogue
Pink Pony Club - Chappell Roan
Rain On Me - Lady Gaga, Ariana Grande
Same Love - Macklemore, Ryan Lewis, Mary Lambert
Secret Love Song - Little Mix, Jason, Derulo
She Is Beauty We Are World Class - Louis Tomlinson
Speak Now (Taylor's Version) - Taylor Swift
THATS WHAT I WANT - Lil Nas X
This Is Me - The Greatest Showman Cast
We R Who We R - Kesha
What I Need - Hayley Kiyoko, Kehlani
When We Were Young (The Logical Song) - D. Guetta, K. Petras
You Make Me Feel (Mighty Reel) - Adam Lambert & Sigala
You Need To Calm Down - Taylor Swift

Join the Wedding MusicLetter for the latest and trending wedding songs - every Wednesday.

MOTOWN WEDDING SONGS

Ceremony
Back At One – Brian McKnight
Endless Love – Lionel Richie, Diana Ross
For Once In My Life – Stevie Wonder
I Believe (When I Fall in Love) - Stevie Wonder
I Believe In You And Me – The Four Tops
Ready for Love - India.Arie
Share My Life – Kem
Signed, Sealed, Delivered (I'm Yours) – Stevie Wonder
Thank God I Found You – Mariah Carey, Joe, 98 Degrees
You're All I Need to Get By – M. Gaye, T. Terrell
Your Precious Love – Marvin Gaye, Tammi Terrell

Cocktail Hour/Reception Background Music
All Night Long - Mary Jane Girls
Baby I Need Your Loving – The Four Tops
Because of You – 98 Degrees
Cruisin' – Smokey Robinson
For The Love Of You – The Isley Brothers
Hey Mr. D.J. - Zhané
How Sweet It Is (To Be Loved by You) – Marvin Gaye
I Heard It Through the Grapevine – Marvin Gaye
I Love Your Smile – Shanice
I Second That Emotion – Smokey Robinson & the Miracles
I Was Made To Love Her – Stevie Wonder
I'll Always Love You – The Spinners
I'll Be There – The Jackson 5
Let's Get Serious - Jermaine Jackson
Lie To Me – Kem
My Guy - Mary Wells
Nightshift - Commodores
Rhythm of the Night - DeBarge

First Dance
Best Thing That Ever Happened To Me – Gladys Knight
I Choose You - Willie Hutch
Love of My Life – Brian McKnight
One In A Million You – Larry Graham
Stuck on You – Lionel Richie
You Are My Lady – Freddie Jackson
You Are the Sunshine of My Life – Stevie Wonder

Slow Dances
All This Love - DeBarge
Just My Imagination (Running Away with Me) – The Temptations
Let's Stay Together - Al Green
Live Out Your Love – Kem, Toni Braxton
My Girl – The Temptations
On Bended Knee – Boyz II Men
Ooo Baby Baby – Smokey Robinson and the Miracles
Still - The Commodores
Three Times A Lady – The Commodores
You Really Got A Hold On Me – Smokey Robinson and the Miracles

Upbeat Dance Songs
Ain't No Mountain High Enough – M. Gaye, T. Terrell
Ain't Nothing Like the Real Thing – M. Gaye, T. Terrell
Ain't That Peculiar – Marvin Gaye
Ain't Too Proud to Beg – The Temptations
All Night Long (All Night) Lionel Richie
Baby Love – The Supremes
Brick House - The Commodores
Dancing in the Street – Martha and the Vandellas
Do You Love Me – The Contours
Get Ready – The Temptations
Heard It Through the Grapevine – Gladys Knight & the Pips
Heatwave - Martha & The Vandellas
I Can't Help Myself – The Four Tops
I Want You Back – The Jackson 5
I Wish – Stevie Wonder
I'm Coming Out - Diana Ross
It Takes Two – Marvin Gaye, Kim Weston
It's the Same Old Song – The Four Tops
Please Mr. Postman – The Marvelettes
Reach Out I'll Be There – The Four Tops
Stop! In the Name of Love – The Supremes
Super Freak - Rick James
Superstition – Stevie Wonder
The Love You Save – The Jackson 5
This Old Heart Of Mine (Is Weak For You) – The Isley Brothers
Uptight (Everything's Alright) – Stevie Wonder
You Can't Hurry Love – The Supremes
You Keep Me Hangin' On – The Supremes

Party-Ending Songs
Cloud Nine – The Temptations
End of the Road - Boyz II Men
Let's Get It On – Marvin Gaye
Never Can Say Goodbye – The Jackson 5
Papa Was a Rollin' Stone – The Temptations
Tracks of My Tears – Smokey Robinson and the Miracles
Where Did Our Love Go – The Supremes

Join the Wedding MusicLetter for the latest and trending wedding songs - every Wednesday.

POP WEDDING SONGS

Ceremony
A Thousand Years - Christina Perri
All You Need Is Love - Katy Perry
Beautiful In White - Shane Filan
Can't Help Falling In Love - Haley Reinhart
I Don't Want to Miss a Thing - Music Travel Love
Marry Me - Jennifer Lopez, Maluma
Marry Me - Train
Ocean - LunchMoney Lewis, Meghan Trainor
Perfect Duet - Ed Sheeran, Beyoncé

Cocktail Hour
A Thousand Miles - Vanessa Carlton
Angel - Shaggy, Rayvon
Be My Forever - Christina Perri, Ed Sheeran
Brighter Than The Sun - Colbie Caillat
Butterflies - MAX, Ali Gatie
Cold Heart (PNAU Remix) - Elton John, Dua Lipa
Count on Me - Bruno Mars
Espresso - Sabrina Carpenter
Everything - Michael Bublé
Everywhere - Fleetwood Mac
Falling - Sophia Annello
Flowers - Miley Cyrus
Fresh Eyes - Andy Grammer
Hold On - Wilson Phillips
I Do - Colbie Caillat
I Like Me Better - Lauv
I Want It That Way - Backstreet Boys
I'm Yours - Jason Mraz
One Step At A Time - Jordin Sparks
Please Please Please - Sabrina Carpenter
Say It Right - Nelly Fertado
Sucker - Jonas Brothers

First Dance
Before You - Benson Boone
Black And White (Stripped) - Niall Horan
First Date (Acoustic) - Taylor Acorn
Heaven - Calum Scott
Imagine (Acoustic) - Ben Platt
Lifetime - Justin Bieber
Love Someone - Lukas Graham
Lover - Taylor Swift
Say You Won't Let Go - James Arthur
Thinking Out Loud - Ed Sheeran
Tuesdays - Jake Scott

Slow Dances
Careless Whisper - George Michael
Die With A Smile - Lady Gaga & Bruno Mars
Fade into You - Mazzy Star
Forever Young - Alphaville
Love On The Brain - Rihanna
Love You Still (abcdefu romantic version) - Tyler Shaw
Truly Madly Deeply - Savage Garden
Until I Found You - Stephen Sanchez

Reception Upbeat & Dance Hits
24K Magic - Bruno Mars
All About That Bass - Meghan Trainor
As It Was - Harry Styles
Believe - Cher
Blank Space (Taylor's Version) - Taylor Swift
Call Me Maybe - Carly Rae Jepsen
Can't Get You Out Of My Head - Kylie Minogue
Can't Stop The Feeling! - Justin Timberlake
Cooler Than Me - Mike Posner
Dance The Night - Dua Lipa
Don't Stop 'Til You Get Enough - Michael Jackson
Everybody (Backstreet's Back) - Backstreet Boys
Fantasy - Mariah Carey
Fireball - Pitbull feat. John Ryan
Girls Just Want To Have Fun - Cyndi Lauper
Give Me Everything - Pitbull
Heaven Is A Place On Earth - Belinda Carlisle
HOT TO GO! - Chappell Roan
Hotel Room Service - Pitbull
I Wanna Dance with Somebody - Whitney Houston
Just Dance - Lady Gaga, Colby O'Donis
Kings & Queens - Ava Max
Levitating - Dua Lipa
Lil Boo Thang - Paul Russell
Party In The U.S.A. - Miley Cyrus
Poker Face - Lady Gaga
Promiscious - Nelly Fertado
Roar - Katy Perry
Sexyback - Justin Timberlake
Shake It Off - Taylor Swift
Shivers - Ed Sheeran
Shut Up and Dance - WALK THE MOON
Sweet Dreams Are Made Of This - Eurythmics
Take On Me - a-Ha
Temperature - Sean Paul
Timber - Pitbull, Ke$ha
Unwritten - Natasha Bedingfield
Uptown Funk - Mark Ronson
Wannabe - Spice Girls
We Found Love - Rihanna & Calvin Harris
Yeah! - Usher, Lil Jon, Ludacris

Grand Exit
Belong Together - Mark Ambor
Bye Bye Bye - *Nsync
Carry You Home - Alex Warren
Counting Stars - OneRepublic
Happy - Pharrell Williams
(I've Had) The Time of My Life - Bill Medley, Jennifer Warnes
Memories - Maroon 5
Never Gonna Give You Up - Rick Astley
Paper Rings - Taylor Swift
Walking On Sunshine - Katrina & The Waves
You Make My Dreams (Come True) - Hall and Oates

Join the Wedding MusicLetter for the latest and trending wedding songs - every Wednesday.

POP-PUNK WEDDING SONGS

Entrance Songs
I Write Sins Not Tragedies - Panic! At The Disco
The Anthem - Good Charlotte
The Middle - Jimmy Eat World
Welcome To The Black Parade - My Chemical Romance

Background Songs (Cocktail Hour, Dinner)
Complicated - Avril Lavigne
If It Means A Lot To You - A Day To Remember
Island In The Sun - Weezer
Perfect - Simple Plan
Wake Me Up When September Ends - Green Day
Your Guardian Angel - The Red Jumpsuit Apparatus

Last Dance Songs
Good Riddance (Time of Your Life) - Green Day
My Friends Over You - New Found Glory
The Great Escape - Boys Like Girls
Thnks fr th Mmrs - Fall Out Boy

Party Dance Songs
1985 - Bowling For Soup
All the Small Things - blink-182
Are You Gonna Be My Girl - Jet
Basket Case - Green Day
Be My Escape - Relient K
Beverly Hills - Weezer
Check Yes, Juliet - We the Kings
Dear Maria, Count Me In - All Time Low
Dirty Little Secret - The All-American Rejects
Face Down - The Red Jumpsuit Apparatus
Fat Lip - Sum 41
First Date - blink-182
Flavor Of The Weak - American Hi-Fi
Gives You Hell - The All-American Rejects
Holiday - Green Day
I'd Do Anything - Simple Plan
I'm Just A Kid - Simple Plan
In Too Deep - Sum 41
Last Resort - Papa Roach
Lifestyles of the Rich & Famous - Good Charlotte
Misery Business - Paramore
Mr. Brightside - The Killers
My Own Worst Enemy - Lit
Ocean Avenue - Yellowcard
Shake It - Metro Station
Sk8er Boi - Avril Lavigne
Smooth Criminal - Alien Ant Farm
Somebody Told Me - The Killers
Stacy's Mom - Fountains of Wayne
Still Into You - Paramore
Sugar, We're Goin Down - Fall Out Boy
Teenagers - My Chemical Romance
Teenage Dirtbag - Wheatus
The Boys of Summer - The Ataris
The Kids Aren't Alright - The Offspring
The Taste of Ink - The Used
What's My Age Again? - blink-182

Join the Wedding MusicLetter for the latest and trending wedding songs - every Wednesday.

R&B WEDDING SONGS

Ceremony (Processional, Recessional, and Vows)
All Of Me – John Legend
At Last – Etta James
Fall For You - Leela James
For You – Kenny Lattimore
Forever – Jaheim
Happily Ever After – Case
I'm Sure It's You (The Wedding Song) – Sheléa
Let's Fall In Love - R. DeVaughn, K. Allen & H.M.P.
Marry Me – Jason Derulo
Marry Your Daughter - Brian McKnight Jr.
Sent From Heaven - Rahsaan Patterson
This Will Be (An Everlasting Love) – Natalie Cole
Today I Do – Tamia

First Dance
All My Life – K-Ci & JoJo
Anything For You (The Duet) - Ledisi, Morton
At My Worst - Pink Sweat$, Kehlani
Best Part - Daniel Caesar feat. H.E.R.
Beyond – Leon Bridges
Consider Me – Allen Stone
Conversations in the Dark - John Legend
Every Kind Of Way - H.E.R.
Find Someone Like You - Snoh Aalegra
Forever – Vedo
Like I'm Gonna Lose You - M. Trainor, J. Legend
Love Of My Life - Brian McKnight
Love You Anyway - Devon Gilfillian
Made For Me - Muni Long
Spend My Life With You – Eric Benet, Tamia
Why I Love You – MAJOR.

Cocktail Hour
4 Me - Don Toliver, Kali Uchis
As a matter of fact - Babyface
Baby Will You Love Me - MAJOR.
Better - Khalid
How Deep Is Your Love - PJ Morton
I Do Love You - G.Q.
Keeps On Fallin' – Babyface, Ella Mai
Killing Me Softly With His Song - Fugees
Kiss Me More - Doja Cat, SZA
Lovely Day - Amber Mark
Never Too Much   Luther Vandross
Saturn - SZA
Set Adrift On Memory Bliss - P.M. Dawn
Skate - Silc Sonic
Smooth Operator - Sade
So In Love – Jill Scott, Anthony Hamilton
That's The Way Love Goes - Janet Jackson
The Best - Tina Turner
U 2 Luv - Ne-Yo, Jeremih
Waterfalls - TLC

Parent Dances
I'll Be There - Jackson 5
Isn't She Lovely – Stevie Wonder
Lean on Me - Bill Withers
Unforgettable – Nat King Cole, Natalie Cole
You Are The Sunshine Of My Life – Stevie Wonder

Slow Dance Songs
Adorn - Miguel
Always and Forever – Heatwave
Bring It On Home to Me - Sam Cooke
Endless Love – Lionel Richie, Diana Ross
Foirever My Lady - Jodeci
Forever Mine – The O'Jays
Here And Now – Luther Vandross
Let's Stay Together – Al Green
My Boo - Alicia Keys & USHER
My Girl - The Temptations
Stand By Me - Ben E. King
Under the Influence - Chris Brown

Party Hits
Ain't No Mountain High Enough - M. Gaye & T. Terrell
Ain't Nobody - Chaka Khan
Before I Let Go - Maze, Frankie Beverly
Billie Jean – Michael Jackson
Brick House – The Commodores
Can't Get Enough - Tamia
Can't Get Enough Of Your Love, Babe – Barry White
Crazy In Love – Beyoncé
DJ Got Us Fallin' In Love - Usher, Pitbull
Everyday People - Sly And The Family Stone
Family Affair - Mary J. Blige
Forever - Chris Brown
Get Down On It - Kool & The Gang
Go Crazy – Chris Brown, Young Thug
I Wanna Be Your Lover – Prince
I Wanna Dance with Somebody – Whitney Houston
I Want You Back - Jackson 5
Let's Get Married (ReMarqable Remix) – Jagged Edge
Let's Groove - Earth Wind & Fire
Love Like This – Faith Evans
Miss Independent - Ne-Yo
No Diggity - Blackstreet and Dr. Dre
One, Two Step - Ciara, Missy Elliott
Party All the Time - Eddie Murphy
Play That Funky Music - Wild Cherry
Poison - Bell Biv Devoe
Pony - Ginuwine
Respect - Aretha Franklin
Return of the Mack – Mark Morrison
September – Earth, Wind & Fire
Superstar - Jamelia
Superstition - Stevie Wonder
This Is How We Do It – Montell Jordan
Too Close – Next

Join the Wedding MusicLetter for the latest and trending wedding songs - every Wednesday.

REGGAE WEDDING SONGS

Romantic and Love Songs
All for You - Stick Figure
All My Life - Marcia Griffiths, DA'Ville
All Of Me - Jah Cure
Always Remember Us This Way - Cris Hagman
Angel - Shaggy
Don't Let Go - Spawnbreezie
Forever More - Alaine, Tarrus Riley
Happy Heart - Etana
I Can't Help, Falling In Love With You - UB40
Is This Love - Bob Marley
La La Means I Love You - Alton Ellis
Life Is Better With You - Michael Franti & Spearhead
Love Has Found Its Way - Dennis Brown
Love Me Easy - ANORA, Stick Figure, Walshy Fire
Marry You - Perfect Giddimani
Only You - Jah Cure feat. Mya
Someone Loves You Honey - J.C. Lodge
There For You - Beres Hammond
Truly - Marcia Griffiths
You're The One I Love - Shenseea, Rvssian

Feel-Good Songs
Baby, I Love Your Way - Big Mountain
Beach In Hawaii - Ziggy Marley
Below The Waist - Queen Ifrica
Close To You - Maxi Priest
Come Over - Estelle ft Sean Paul
Could You Be Loved - Bob Marley
Don't Worry, Be Happy - Bobby McFerrin
Edge of the Ocean - Stick Figure
Every Night Every Morning - Maoli
Everything I Own - Ken Boothe
Girls Dem Sugar - Beenie Man, Mya
Have It All (Reggae Mix) - Jason Mraz
I am Blessed - Mr. Vegas
I Feel Good - Beres Hammond
I Got You - Michael Franti & Spearhead
I Love My Life - Demarco
I Love You Too - Ziggy Marley
Love and Affection - Pressure
Love Me - Fia
Love You Right - Morgan Heritage
No Ordinary Love - Alaine
Praise Jah In the Moonlight - YG Marley
Real Love - Lloyd Brown
Red Red Wine - UB40
Rise in Love - Alaine
Rockaway - Beres Hammond
Rumor - Maoli
She's Royal - Tarrus Riley
Smile - WizKid, H.E.R.
Soul Provider - Romain Virgo
Three Little Birds - Bob Marley & The Wailers
Way of Life - Stick Figure, Slightly Stoopid
Welcome to Jamrock - Damian Marley
You and Me - SOJA, Chris Boomer

Upbeat and Dance Hits
Action - Terror Fabulous, Nadine Sutherland
Anything For You - Snow & Friends
Beautiful - Seeed
Boom Shack-A-Lak - Apache Indian
Boombastic - Shaggy
Calling On Me - Sean Paul, Tove Lo
Down Under - Men At Work
Electric Avenue - Eddy Grant
Get Busy - Sean Paul
Gyal You A Party Animal - Charly Black
Here Comes The Hotstepper - Ini Kamoze
Hold You (Hold Yuh) - Gyptian
I Like To Move It - Reel 2 Real
Iko Iko (My Bestie) - Justin Wellington feat. Small Jam
Informer - Snow
It Wasn't Me - Shaggy feat. Ricardo Ducent
Murder She Wrote - Chaka Demus And Pliers
No Games - Serani
No Letting Go - Wayne Wonder
No Lie - Sean Paul, Dua Lipa
Pon de Replay - Rihanna
Pon De River Pon De Bank - Elephant Man
Rum & Redbull - Beenie Man, Future Fambo
Say Hey (I Love You) - Michael Franti & Spearhead
Shy Guy - Diana King
Speechless - J'calm
Temperature - Sean Paul
That Girl - Maxi Priest, Shaggy
Toast - Koffee
Turn Me On - Kevin Lyttle
Walking Trophy - Hoodcelebrityy
Who Am I? (Sim Simma) - Beenie Man

Classic and Iconic Reggae
All I Have Is Love - Gregory Isaacs
Bam Bam - Sister Nancy
Cherry Oh Baby - Eric Donaldson
Good Thing Going - Sugar Minott
Here I Come - Barrington Levy
I Can See Clearly Now - Jimmy Cliff
I Want To Wake Up With You - Boris Gardiner
I'll Do Anything for You - Denroy Morgan
Melody Life - Marcia Griffiths
My Boy Lollipop - Millie
Night Nurse - Gregory Isaacs
One Love/People Get Ready - Bob Marley
Sitting & Watching - Dennis Brown
Tempted To Touch - Beres Hammond

Fun & Novelty
Bad Boys - Inner Circle
Banana Boat (Day-O) - Harry Belafonte
Electric Boogie - Marcia Griffiths
I'm Getting Married - Yellowman

Join the Wedding MusicLetter for the latest and trending wedding songs - every Wednesday.

ROCK WEDDING SONGS

Ceremony
All I Want Is You - U2
Bittersweet Symphony - The Verve
Chasing Cars - Snow Patrol
Everlong (Acoustic) - Foo Fighters
Here Comes The Sun - The Beatles
ILYSB - LANY
Turning Page - Sleeping At Last
Best Day Of My Life - American Authors
Dog Days Are Over - Florence + the Machine
Home - Edward Sharpe & The Magnetic Zeros
I'll Follow You into the Dark - Death Cab For Cutie
If I Didn't Have You - BANNERS
On Top Of The World - Imagine Dragons
You and Me - Lifehouse

Cocktail Hour
Africa - Toto
All Summer Long - Kid Rock
BIRDS OF A FEATHER - Billie Eilish
broken - lovelytheband
Come and Get Your Love - Redbone
Dancing in the Moonlight - King Harvest
Everywhere - Fleetwood Mac
feelslikeimfallinginlove - Coldplay
Friday I'm in Love - The Cure
Good Together - Lake Street Dive
Heat Waves - Glass Animals
I Think I Like You - The Band CAMINO
I'm In Love With You - The 1975
Let My Love Open The Door - Pete Townshend
New Light - John Mayer
Out Of My League - Fitz & The Tantrums
What's Up? - 4 Non Blondes
Wonderwall - Oasis

First Dance
All Because of You - O.A.R.
All I Want Is You - The Decemberists
(Everything I Do) I Do It For You - Bryan Adams
Fall for You - Secondhand Serenade
Forever - Ben Harper
Nothing Else Matters - Metallica
Tangled Up In You - Staind
Wherever You Will Go - The Calling
You're The One - Black Keys
You're The One - Greta Van Fleet

Slow Dance Songs
I Don't Want To Miss A Thing - Aerosmith
Faithfully - Journey
Wonderful Tonight - Eric Clapton
I Want to Know What Love Is - Foreigner
Iris - The Goo Goo Dolls
Your Song - Elton John
Tonight, Tonight - The Smashing Pumpkins
Just the Way You Are - Billy Joel

Upbeat Dance Songs
All Star - Smash Mouth
Blister In The Sun - Violent Femmes
Bohemian Rhapsody - Queen
Brown Eyed Girl - Van Morrison
Come On Eileen - Dexy's Midnight Runners
Dancing In the Dark - Bruce Springsteen
Don't Stop Believin' - Journey
Don't Stop Me Now - Queen
Ex's & Oh's - Elle King
Footloose - Kenny Loggins
How You Remind Me - Nickelback
I Love Rock 'N Roll - Joan Jett & the Blackhearts
I Ran (So Far Away) - A Flock Of Seagulls
Lips Like Sugar - by Echo And The Bunnymen
Livin' On A Prayer - Bon Jovi
Mr. Blue Sky - Electric Light Orchestra
One Week - Barenaked Ladies
Rich Girl - Daryl Hall & John Oates
Shut Up and Dance - Walk The Moon
Smooth - Santana feat. Rob Thomas
Summer Of '69 - Bryan Adams
Sweet Dreams (Are Made Of This) - Eurythmics
Sweet Home Alabama - Lynyrd Skynyrd
Tongue Tied - GROUPLOVE
Twist And Shout - The Beatles
We Are Young - Fun. feat. Janelle Monáe
Welcome To The Jungle - Guns N' Roses
You Shook Me All Night Long - AC/DC
Your Love - Outfield

Party Anthems (Late Night)
A-Punk - Vampire Weekend
bad guy - Billie Eilish
Born For This - The Score
Bring Me to Life - Evanescence
Good 4 U - Olivia Rodrigo
High Hopes - Panic! At the Disco
Higher - Creed
I Believe in a Thing Called Love - The Darkness
In the End - LINKIN PARK
Kryptonite - 3 Doors Down
Semi-Charmed Life - Third Eye Blind
Seven Nation Army - The White Stripes
Someone To You - BANNERS
Use Somebody - Kings of Leon

Exit Songs (Last Dance or Grand Exit)
A Sky Full of Stars - Coldplay
Don't You (Forget About Me) - Simple Minds
I'll Be There For You - The Rembrandts
Let's Get Married - Bleachers
Piano Man - Billy Joel
Stargazing - Myles Smith
Take Me Home Tonight - Eddie Money
Thunderstruck - AC/DC

SING-ALONG SONGS

Classic Singalong Anthems
Bohemian Rhapsody - Queen
Brown Eyed Girl - Van Morrison
Don't Stop Believin' - Journey
If I Could Turn Back Time - Cher
Jack & Diane - John Mellencamp
Livin' On A Prayer - Bon Jovi
My Way - Frank Sinatra
Ob-La-Di, Ob-La-Da - The Beatles
Paradise by the Dashboard Light - Meat Loaf
Somebody To Love - Queen
Sweet Caroline - Neil Diamond
Y.M.C.A. - Village People

Pop Hits & Party Starters
A Thousand Miles - Vanessa Carlton
Baby - Justin Bieber
Big Girls Don't Cry (Personal) - Fergie
Bye Bye Bye - *NSYNC
Call Me Maybe - Carly Rae Jepsen
Classic - MKTO
Dancing On My Own - Robyn
Hold On - Wilson Phillips
Hot To Go! - Chappell Roan
I Kissed A Girl - Katy Perry
I Wanna Dance With Somebody - Whitney Houston
I Want It That Way - Backstreet Boys
It's All Coming Back To Me Now - Celine Dion
Just The Way You Are - Bruno Mars
Love Song - Sara Bareilles
Party In The U.S.A. - Miley Cyrus
Roar - Katy Perry
Shake It Off - Taylor Swift
Shape Of You - Ed Sheeran
Story Of My Life - One Direction
Tonight Tonight - Hot Chelle Rae
Unwritten - Natasha Bedingfield
Wannabe - Spice Girls
We Are Young - .fun, Janelle Monáe

Rock & Alternative
All Summer Long - Kid Rock
Complicated - Avril Lavigne
Everybody Talks - Neon Trees
Fresh Eyes - Andy Grammer
Hey, Soul Sister - Train
How Bizarre - OMC
I'm A Believer - Smash Mouth
I'm Gonna Be (500 Miles) - The Proclaimers
Ironic - Alanis Morissette
Mr. Brightside - The Killers
Piano Man - Billy Joel
Stacy's Mom - Bowling For Soup
Use Somebody - Kings Of Leon
What's Up? - 4 Non Blondes/DJ Miko

Romantic & Emotional
Clarity - Zedd, Foxes
Just Give Me A Reason - Pink, Nate Ruess
My Life Would Suck Without You - Kelly Clarkson
No Air - Jordin Sparks, Chris Brown
Symphony - Clean Bandit, Zara Larsson

Country & Folk
Budapest - George Ezra
Can't Fight The Moolight - LeAnn Rimes
Fast Car - Tracy Chapman
Friends In Low Places - Garth Brooks
I Will Wait - Mumford & Sons
Man! I Feel Like A Woman! - Shania Twain
Take Me Home, Country Roads - John Denver
The Devil Went Down to Georgia - Charlie Daniels
The Gambler - Kenny Rogers
This Kiss - Faith Hill

R&B, Hip-Hop & Dance Hits
99 Problems - Jay-Z
All I Do Is Win - DJ Khaled
Crazy - Gnarls Barkley
DJ Got Us Falling In Love - Usher, Pitbull
Down - Jay Sean, Lil Wayne
Fantasy - Mariah Carey
Fight For Your Right - Beastie Boys
Hotel Room Service - Pitbull
It Wasn't Me - Shaggy, Rik Rok
Killing Me Softly With His Song - The Fugees
Let Me Love You - Mario
Lose Yourself - Eminem
No Diggity - Blackstreet & Dr. Dre & Queen Pen
No Scrubs - TLC
Pony - Ginuwine
Promiscuous - Nelly Furtado, Timbaland
Put Your Records On - Corinne Bailey Rae
Right Here (Human Nature Remix) - SWV
Timber - Pitbull, Kesha
Want You To Want Me - Jason Derulo

Feel-Good & Inspirational Tunes
A Million Dreams - Pink
Believer - Imagine Dragons
Born This Way - Lady Gaga
Dynamite - Taio Cruz
Feeling Good - Michael Bublé
Fire Burning - Sean Kingston
Girl on Fire - Alicia Keys
Good Feeling - Flo Rida
Stronger - Kanye West
Wake Me Up - Avicii

Join the Wedding MusicLetter for the latest and trending wedding songs - every Wednesday.

TEXAS COUNTRY & RED DIRT

Prelude/Processional
All the Way – Shane Smith & the Saints
Feet Don't Touch The Ground – Stoney LaRue
I Cross My Heart – George Strait
I Love You – Eli Young Band
I'll Never Stop Loving You – Jay Eric, Brandi Behlen
In His Arms – Jack Ingram, M. Lambert, J. Randall
In Your Love - Tyler Childers
Keep You Forever – Erick Willis
Love You For Loving Me – Stoney LaRue
Next To Heaven – Aaron Watson
On My Way To You – Cody Johnson
Promise You Me – Grant Gilbert
Sent Me You – Josh Ward
Walk in a Room - Muscadine Bloodline
When I Said I Do – Clint Black, Lisa Hartman Black
You (Wedding Song) – Jason Cassidy
Yours and Mine – Kyle Park

Recessional
Backroad Song – Granger Smith
Happens Like That – Granger Smith
I Won't Give Up – Randy Rogers Band
Lady May - Tyler Childers
My Church – Maren Morris
Settle Me Down – Josh Abbott Band
She's All Mine – Cody Jinks
Wave On Wave – Pat Green

Cocktail Hour
Bluebird – Miranda Lambert
Buy Myself A Chance – Randy Rogers Band
Check Yes Or No – George Strait
Drinkin' Problem – Midland
Kiss Me – Casey Donahew
Kiss Me In The Dark – Randy Rogers Band
Long Hot Summer Day – Turnpike Troubadour
Luckenbach, Texas – Waylon Jennings
Oh, Tonight – Josh Abbott Band feat. Kacey Musgraves
You and Me and the Neon – The Western Express

Dinner
Burn, Burn, Burn - Zach Bryan
Give You A Ring – Casey Donahew
In Color – Jamey Johnson
Keep The Wolves Away – Uncle Lucius
Pretty Heart – Parker McCollum
She Won't Be Lonely Long – Clay Walker
Southside of Heaven – Ryan Bingham
The Bones – Maren Morris
The House That Built Me – Miranda Lambert
There Was This Girl - Riley Green
Wicked Twisted Road – Reckless Kelly
You Can Have The Crown – Sturgill Simpson

First Dance
10-90 - Muscadine Bloodline
All Your'n – Tyler Childers
Beautiful Crazy – Luke Combs
Cover Me Up – Jason Isbell
Crazy Girl – Eli Young Band
Dance of a Lifetime - Drake Milligan
I Don't Wanna Go To Heaven – Nate Smith
I Just Wanna Be Yours – Full Throttle
I'm Gonna Love You – Logan Mize
Love In The First Degree – Wade Bowen, Brandy Clark
One Woman – Randy Rogers Band
Steady Heart – Kameron Marlowe
Texas Angel – Honeybrowne
Who I Am – Wade Bowen
Who I Am With You – Chris Young

Dance Party
All I See Is You – Shane Smith & the Saints
Diamond In My Pocket – Cody Johnson
Feathered Indians - Tyler Childers
Horses Are Faster - Ian Munsick
Howdy to Here - Ty Walker
If I Could Make A Living – Clay Walker
Killin' Time – Clint Black
Me On You - Muscadine Bloodline
More Girls Like You – Kip Moore
Night Shift - Jon Pardi
No Vacancy - Treaty Oak Revival
One in a Lifetime Girl – Micky And The Motorcars
Somethin' 'Bout A Truck - Kip Moore
Something To Talk About – Koe Wetzel
Song of the South - Alabama
Sounds Like the Radio - Zach Top
Stronger Than A Storm - Dylan Gossett
The Luckiest – Josh Abbott Band
Time Marches On – Tracy Lawrence
We Ride - Bryan Martin

Slow Dances
Broken Window Serenade – Whiskey Myers
Carrying Your Love With Me - George Strait
Fall In Love – Bailey Zimmerman
Hurricane – The Band of Heathens
Loud and Heavy – Cody Jinks
Millionaire - Chris Stapleton
Neon Moon - Brooks & Dunn
Ride the Lightning (717 Tapes) – Warren Zeiders
Sand In My Boots - Morgan Wallen
Save Me - Jelly Roll
Something In The Orange - Zach Bryan
Why – Read Southall Band

Last Dance/Send-off
Best For Last – Aaron Watson
Burn Out – Midland
Dance Her Home – Cody Johnson
Revival - Zach Bryan
Suitcase – Steve Moakler
This Damn Song – Pecos & the Rooftops
Traveler - Chris Stapleton
Until I Met You – Sundy Best

WEDDING MUSIC DETAILS

Favorite Style of Music:

Grand Entrance Introductions:

Preferred background music theme:

First Dance Song:

Parent Dances:

Other Formal Dances:

Cake Cutting Song:

Bouquet Toss & Garter Toss:

Longest Married Dance:

Last Dance and/or Private Last Dance:

Do any songs have special meaning? (alma mater, playing when you met, etc)

Notes:

Join the Wedding MusicLetter for the latest and trending wedding songs - every Wednesday.

WEDDING DETAILS

Couple's Names:

Ceremony Location:

Ceremony Start Time:

Reception Location:

Reception Start Time:

Reception End Time:

Expected Number of Guests:

Indoors or Outdoors?

Notes:

Join the Wedding MusicLetter for the latest and trending wedding songs - every Wednesday.

WEDDING PLANNING NOTES

My Notes:

Join the Wedding MusicLetter for the latest and trending wedding songs - every Wednesday.

ABOUT THE AUTHOR

Matt Campbell began as a mobile DJ business owner in Montana in 1993 DJ Express. His love of music and weddings continued while performing at hundreds of weddings, parties, and school dances for seven years. In early 2000, Matt moved to Las Vegas, Nevada to be with his future bride. In 2024, they celebrated their 22nd wedding anniversary.

My Wedding Songs (MyWeddingSongs.com) was born in 2017 with the mission of offering engaged couples, DJs, and wedding pros popular and unique wedding song ideas. Through the years, My Wedding Songs has grown to hundreds of playlists including for the ceremony and reception, music artists, eras, genres, cultural, and dance styles. The website has helped more than 25 million visitors plan their wedding music! Wowzers!

I hope you were able to find the songs you needed to make your wedding day uniquely yours. Music will set the mood and atmosphere of your entire wedding day. When it's time to party, have every guest singing their heart out, sweating from dancing, and enjoying a special moment with a loved one during a slow dance.

THANK YOU!

Wishing you all the best!

Matthew Campbell
hello@myweddingsongs.com

Join the Wedding MusicLetter for the latest and trending wedding songs - every Wednesday.

Made in the USA
Columbia, SC
23 October 2024